Speculating on the Edge of Psychoanalysis

In *Speculating on the Edge of Psychoanalysis*, Pablo Lerner questions, and takes a step beyond, the prevailing paradigm of Lacanian psychoanalysis and its emphasis on the sovereignty of language and *jouissance*.

Arguing for the existence of a primordial real void outside and independent of language, Lerner re-thinks the structure and functioning of Lacan's three orders and their complex interrelations. Silence, darkness, and emptiness are the names of the voids within the symbolic, the imaginary, and the real, and, in the gaps between these orders, the voids converge. Thus, Lerner re-conceptualizes the fundamental structure of the field of subjectivity, offering radical and original perspectives on a diverse range of psychoanalytical, philosophical, and theological topics. Chapters span themes such as creation and poetry, death and solitude, intuition and mysticism, truth and being, pantheism and polytheism, the poetic art of interpretation, and introduces a new mathematical conceptualization of psychoanalytic metapsychology and the clinical structures.

This volume offers new psychoanalytic perspectives of great interest for practitioners and scholars in the fields of psychoanalysis, philosophy, theology, and literary studies.

Pablo Lerner is a psychologist and psychoanalyst based in Paris, France, offering psychoanalytic psychotherapies in private practice.

The Lines of the Symbolic in Psychoanalysis Series
Series Editor:
Ian Parker, Manchester Psychoanalytic Matrix

Psychoanalytic clinical and theoretical work is always embedded in specific linguistic and cultural contexts and carries their traces, traces which this series attends to in its focus on multiple contradictory and antagonistic 'lines of the Symbolic'. This series takes its cue from Lacan's psychoanalytic work on three registers of human experience, the Symbolic, the Imaginary and the Real, and employs this distinctive understanding of cultural, communication and embodiment to link with other traditions of cultural, clinical and theoretical practice beyond the Lacanian symbolic universe. The Lines of the Symbolic in Psychoanalysis Series provides a reflexive reworking of theoretical and practical issues, translating psychoanalytic writing from different contexts, grounding that work in the specific histories and politics that provide the conditions of possibility for its descriptions and interventions to function. The series makes connections between different cultural and disciplinary sites in which psychoanalysis operates, questioning the idea that there could be one single correct reading and application of Lacan. Its authors trace their own path, their own line through the Symbolic, situating psychoanalysis in relation to debates which intersect with Lacanian work, explicating it, extending it and challenging it.

Lacanian Fantasy
The Image, Language and Uncertainty
Kirk Turner

Psychoanalysis and the New Rhetoric
Freud, Burke, Lacan, and Philosophy's Other Scenes
Daniel Adleman and Chris Vanderwees

Speculating on the Edge of Psychoanalysis
Rings and Voids
Pablo Lerner

For more information about the series, please visit: https://www.routledge.com/The-Lines-of-the-Symbolic-in-Psychoanalysis-Series/book-series/KARNLOS

Speculating on the Edge of Psychoanalysis

Rings and Voids

Pablo Lerner

LONDON AND NEW YORK

Designed cover image: Amguy / Getty Images

First published 2024
by Routledge
4 Park Square, Milton Park, Abingdon, Oxon OX14 4RN

and by Routledge
605 Third Avenue, New York, NY 10158

Routledge is an imprint of the Taylor & Francis Group, an informa business

© 2024 Pablo Lerner

The right of Pablo Lerner to be identified as author of this work has been asserted in accordance with sections 77 and 78 of the Copyright, Designs and Patents Act 1988.

All rights reserved. No part of this book may be reprinted or reproduced or utilised in any form or by any electronic, mechanical, or other means, now known or hereafter invented, including photocopying and recording, or in any information storage or retrieval system, without permission in writing from the publishers.

Trademark notice: Product or corporate names may be trademarks or registered trademarks, and are used only for identification and explanation without intent to infringe.

British Library Cataloguing-in-Publication Data
A catalogue record for this book is available from the British Library

Library of Congress Cataloging-in-Publication Data
Names: Lerner, Pablo (Psychologist), author.
Title: Speculating on the edge of psychoanalysis : rings and voids / Pablo Lerner.
Description: Abingdon, Oxon ; New York : Routledge, 2024. | Includes bibliographical references and index. |
Identifiers: LCCN 2023004500 (print) | LCCN 2023004501 (ebook) | ISBN 9781032244778 (paperback) | ISBN 9781032244785 (hardback) | ISBN 9781003278740 (ebook)
Subjects: LCSH: Lacan, Jacques, 1901–1981. | Psychoanalysis.
Classification: LCC BF173 .L3528 2024 (print) | LCC BF173 (ebook) | DDC 150.19/5—dc23/eng/20230131
LC record available at https://lccn.loc.gov/2023004500
LC ebook record available at https://lccn.loc.gov/2023004501

ISBN: 978-1-032-24478-5 (hbk)
ISBN: 978-1-032-24477-8 (pbk)
ISBN: 978-1-003-27874-0 (ebk)

DOI: 10.4324/9781003278740

Typeset in Times New Roman
by codeMantra

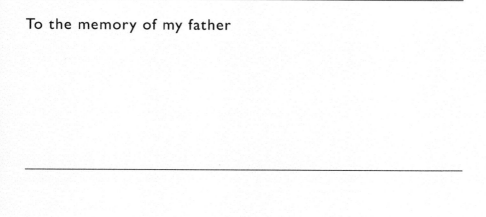

To the memory of my father

Contents

	Series Preface	ix
	Introduction	1
1	Within Without: On Exile and Cosmogony	2
2	Notes on Play	14
3	The End of Grief	24
4	On God and Gods I: Truth and Being	41
5	On God and Gods II: Spinoza, Author of the *Ethics*	61
6	Blahblahcan *avico* Vico	70
7	Ring/ring	89
8	From Beyond the Real	97
	References	*105*
	Index	*109*

Series Preface

This book takes you up steep steps. Rest awhile to reflect on what Pablo Lerner speculates about Heidegger, Vico, and Spinoza, among others, and how they intersect, and do not do so, with Freud and Lacan. The sense in which each of these resources are proto-psychoanalytic, and set the philosophical-theological conditions for psychoanalysis, accumulates with each chapter, and so it is as if you arrive at the top of a pyramid, able to survey the world and what we have made, as if knowing it from within a metalanguage. But that is not possible, and you have been warned many times along the way that this supposed privileged position is illusory.

Or, this book takes you down steep steps, and you go tumbling down, and you will have to grasp hold of a vantage point every now and again, take breath before you fall further. And, if that is the journey you experience yourself taking into the book, you will arrive at a deepest point, emptiness, and abyss. It is there that you encounter what it is to be a finite being and what the lure of God is concerned with, with you. But that is also impossible, going down into the abyss is a mirror-image of climbing a pyramid. Very appropriately so, and also a representation of the world and its representations of the world and what lies beyond it that is specifically warned against.

There is a void. This book is about the void and what we do with it, what we construct around it. It is precisely, and elegantly in this account, organized around three rings which Lacanian psychoanalysts will already, as this sentence unrolls, suspect to be familiar to them: real, imaginary, and symbolic. You are told at the beginning of the book that the void pertaining to the real is primordial, emptiness, that voids in the imaginary are full of emptiness, darkness, and that voids full of emptiness in the symbolic are to be conceptualized as silence.

To sense that you are familiar with something is, as Lacanians will well know, to be led into error, and error, and truth through error, is crucial to this book. Do not imagine that you will directly apprehend the world or what lies outside it, what is unimaginable, and do not be drawn unwittingly too quickly into the crafted text that you will now read. The book renders the imaginary and the symbolic into something unfamiliar, all the better to speculate about the relationship between the imaginary, the symbolic, and the real.

You will be exiled from what you know, and that will enable you to appreciate the force of the proposals unveiled in the course of the book, that the three rings so central to Lacan's work may be considered not so much as topological as algebraic. What are rings? Does that ring true?

Psychoanalytic clinical and theoretical work circulates through multiple intersecting antagonistic symbolic universes. This series opens connections between different cultural sites in which Lacanian work has developed in distinctive ways, in forms of work that question the idea that there could be single correct reading and application. The Lines of the Symbolic in Psychoanalysis Series provides a reflexive reworking of psychoanalysis that transmits Lacanian writing from around the world, steering a course between the temptations of a metalanguage and imaginary reduction, between the claim to provide a god's eye view of psychoanalysis and the idea that psychoanalysis must everywhere be the same. And the elaboration of psychoanalysis in the symbolic here grounds its theory and practice in the history and politics of the work in a variety of interventions that touch the real.

Ian Parker
Manchester Psychoanalytic Matrix

Introduction

The idea of this book is, in a sense, very simple. It concerns rings and voids.

There is only one void, and that void is real. It exists in its own right. It is not an effect of the signifier. It is not an effect of the image. It is primordial. I will call it emptiness.

There are voids in the imaginary, voids full of emptiness. I will call them darkness.

There are voids in the symbolic, voids full of emptiness. I will call them silence.

Silence, darkness, emptiness.

The voids are three, yet they are one. Tripartition of one equal to one. They are inseparable, they pass over into each other continuously. They merge, converge, diverge.

There is only emptiness. It manifests itself by not manifesting itself, by rising up to the surface, in the voids of the surface, as silence, as darkness.

There is the real, the symbolic, the imaginary. They are rings. They are incomplete, full of voids. They are discontinuous. There are disjunctions between them. They never converge. They always diverge. They are always three, never one.

Between them, in their disjunctions, there are voids.

In the disjunction of the imaginary and the symbolic, darkness and silence converge.

In the disjunction of the real and the symbolic, emptiness and silence converge.

In the disjunction of the real and the imaginary, emptiness and darkness converge.

In the center of it all, where the real, the imaginary, and the symbolic diverge, emptiness, darkness, and silence converge.

This is the nature of the unconscious.

Chapter 1

Within Without
On Exile and Cosmogony

On March 31, 1492, the Catholic Monarchs of Spain, Isabella of Castile and Ferdinand II of Aragon, issued the Alhambra Decree, an edict forcing the Sephardim – the Jewish population of Spain – to either convert to Catholicism, leave the country, or face execution without trial. So began yet another chapter in the seemingly never-ending exodus of the Jewish community.

The Sephardic society, from the early thirteenth century onwards, was the center of the radical developments within Judaic mysticism, a process culminating in the writing, distribution, and study of the *Zohar*, the most fundamental work of the Kabbalah. Hence, within the banished Jewish community in Spain, a well-developed mystical circle found itself in a situation closely resembling the mythical historical existential conditions of the Jews – a fact that would have profound consequences for the subsequent development of the Kabbalah.

During the decades following the Decree, the Sephardic Jews spread and settled around Europe, North Africa, and the Middle East. By the middle of the sixteenth century, Sephardic Jews constituted more than half of the population of Safed, a small town in the Upper Galilee, which would become the center of the revolutionary transformations of Jewish mysticism induced by the experience of exile. The most important and influential figure amongst the mystics of Safed was Rabbi Isaac Luria (1534–1572), and the magnitude of the impact that the expulsion from Spain had on Luria's mystical thinking cannot be overestimated. Not only did Luria situate exile at the heart of the historical fate and purpose of the Jewish community, but he also saw it as the most essential moment of the creation of the world.[1]

According to the Kabbalah, God, in his innermost essence, is nothing other than *Ein Sof*, often translated as "the infinite". *Ein Sof* is without determinations, limits, attributes; it is undifferentiated and divine being, impossible to know or represent. It is the *Deus absconditus* of the Hebrew Bible (Isaiah 45:15), the hidden God that remains reticent even in his worldly manifestations and material creation. In essence, *Ein Sof* is absolute being in its unimaginable state before the creation of the world; or with the words from the *Zohar*:

> In the beginning, shape and form having not yet been created, He had neither form nor similitude. Hence it is forbidden to one apprehending him as he is

DOI: 10.4324/9781003278740-2

before Creation, to imagine him under any kind of form or shape ... not either by his complete holy Name, nor by letter or sign of any kind ... nothing which you could embody into a finite conception.[2]

Isaac Luria's conception of the creation of the world proceeds from this view of *Ein Sof* and its paradoxical simultaneous immanence in and absence from the material world. In the beginning – or rather, before it – there was only *Ein Sof*: continuous featurelessness, infinite compactness without limitations or differences. To explain how God could create a finite and differentiated world out of infinite plenitude, Luria introduced the concept of *Tzimtzum*, literally "constriction", "condensation", or "contraction". *Tzimtzum* signifies the process whereby *Ein Sof* withdrew from one region of himself and took shelter in another, thereby leaving behind a finite empty space (*Khalal*) within himself in which creation could take place according to his Will: to make a world in the image of an original, sudden, intuited flash of wisdom (*Chochmah*). In other words, the creation of the world is essentially conceived not as *creatio ex nihilo*, of God directing his creative powers outwards, making the material world out of nothing, but rather as a primordial exile *within* himself,[3] leaving a "nothing" behind in which he could create the universe by filling its darkness with his divine light.

It would certainly be naive to argue that there is any linear causality between the "external" historical exile of the Sephardic Jews and Isaac Luria's cosmogonic myth about the "internal" exile of God; it does, however, raise several arduous questions of interest to psychoanalysis and the psychoanalyst. First, there arises the question about the fourfold division of the signifier "exile": broadly speaking, between voluntary, forced, internal, and external exile, and, more specifically, as in the case of the Sephardim and Luria, between real forced-external (expulsion) and subjective voluntary-internal (*Tzimtzum*) exile. Second, this question may be metaphorized and raised to a metapsychological level, given that the site of the exile is not necessarily conceived in relation to a real or historical territory or event, but as something taking place in relation to the symbolic order of the community in which the subject resides. Third, there arises the question about any hypothetical link between inner exile and creation, a process for which Luria's myth may serve as an allegory; more specifically, the question about the relation between withdrawal, the void it gives rise to, and the process of creation – and, even more radically, about the relation between *Tzimtzum* and what we could call subjective cosmogony, understood as the creation of a world that psychoanalysis many times refers to as "inner". Fourth, and given that the points above give rise to fruitful results, we are confronted with their implications for the conditions of *ars interpretandi* in the clinical situation, especially if interpretation is understood as an act of creation and not only as a product of the analyst's knowledge.

External Exile

I have introduced three concepts signifying voids inscribed in each of Lacan's three orders: the real, the symbolic, and the imaginary. A void in the symbolic order – an inscribed region where there are no signifiers, only the absence of the Other – I call *silence*; a void in the imaginary – where there are no images, only the non-presence of the other – I call *darkness*; a void in the real – where nothing ex-sists – I call *emptiness*. Furthermore, the separation of the three orders is topically represented by these voids as follows: in the disjunction of the symbolic and the imaginary, where the orders drift apart or diverge, silence and darkness converge; in the disjunction of the symbolic and the real, silence and emptiness converge; in the disjunction of the imaginary and the real, darkness and emptiness converge. Given that the "from where?" of the exile is understood as the symbolic order, its "to where?" may be reformulated in terms of these voids. The question "what is exile?" could, on a metaphorical level, be answered as follows: a departure from the symbolic to a void; and its nature, in addition to the dichotomies voluntary-forced and internal-external, could be specified by the question "to which void?"

First, it must be underlined that there is always a subjective moment, or "activity", in forced exile, as is evident, for example, in the external exile of Oedipus after his banishment from Thebe by Creon; we could speak about this form of exile as a "forced choice".[4] Similarly, it could be argued that there is always a "forced" aspect of voluntary exile, as in the case of Antigone, or when violence, political repression, or poverty is at hand, this also being true in less "urgent" cases, as in the voluntary-external exile of Stephen Dedalus in James Joyce's *A Portrait of the Artist as a Young Man*.

Second, I would argue that external exile in general should be understood primarily as a departure from the symbolic towards silence; it is an exit from the symbolic to an "outside" that is, in fact, within the symbolic thus abandoned. In external exile, the subject loses its point of anchorage in the symbolic of the original community; the laws, values, and norms are no longer "automatically" effectuated through the symbolic exchange of everyday life; the link between speaker and listener is broken, thus the functioning of discourse and language is significantly hindered. In short, external exile is primarily characterized by the absence of the Other, by the presence of a hole in the field of the Other threatening its very functioning, and the subject is thrown into the rift of silence, forcing him to confront many of the questions concerning the symbolic which characterize the fate of the exiled: the gap between languages, the confusion of tongues, the ineffaceable genealogical traces in the accent, the subtleness of deciding how to pronounce one's own name; the disorientation felt at the threshold of the symbolic juridical-bureaucratic structures, and the arduous struggles for recognition, rights, and citizenship; the endeavors to recreate the abandoned symbolic order through symbols and practices, the search for a new home, as well as all the complex phenomena pertaining to the diaspora; the identity crisis induced by the reconfiguration of the points of reference of the ego ideal; the forced choice between cultural "assimilation", "adaption", or "fidelity"; survivor's guilt, melancholic nostalgia, and the actual relation to and communication with the country of origin; the questions about transgenerational transmission; the problem of "double exclusion", of racism within the new community and condemnation from the country of origin;

the rejection of signifier representing the subject in the Other, resulting in a loss of symbolic recognition and a depreciation of the value of its speech, et cetera.[5] All of these problems clearly regard the severe crisis of the symbolic order caused by the external exile, the symbolic *disorder* which revolves around the question of the link to the communities, and, more fundamentally, the different indirect effects of the presence of the absence of the Other; hence, we may understand external exile essentially as an exile *with* the absence of the Other, for the subject always carries with him the absence of that which he left behind – the Other is always present as absent-absence-split.

Internal Exile and Creation

Internal exile, however, is a phenomenon that is much more difficult to grasp, not least because of its evident metaphorical nature and the multitude of possible interpretations of it – indeed, it could be argued that internal exile *as such* can only be grasped through metaphors that are irrevocably inadequate, since it is a process, as we will see, in which "words fail". Hence, I will take the liberty of putting forward a psychoanalytic interpretation of Luria's myth of internal exile and cosmogony.

In his seventh seminar, alluding to St. John (John 1:1), Lacan says: "In the beginning was the Word, which is to say, the signifier ... This is all it takes to introduce the dimension of the *ex nihilo* into the structure of the analytical field".[6] Lacan loosely follows the prevalent scholastic interpretation of the creation myth of the Hebrew Bible, according to which God, by articulating the Word ("Let there be light!"), created the world out of nothing; however, he also turns the myth on its head, arguing that "the fashioning of the signifier and the introduction of a gap or a hole in the real are identical",[7] that is, only the signifier can create a hole in the real in which creation may take place. In other words, there is no hole in the real until the creation of the signifier: the *creatio* of the signifier creates the *nihil* in the real.

This may be contrasted to Luria's myth, where there are several significant moments before the beginning of the world understood as the enunciation of the Word. There is a rather precise overlap between the Kabbalah's conception of *Ein Sof* and Lacan's conception of the real: both are unimaginable, unnameable, undifferentiated, and without form; absolute plenitude without difference, limitation, absence. The primordial hole (*Khalal*) in the real (*Ein Sof*), however, is *not* created by the Word, but by an inner exile (*Tzimtzum*), or withdrawal, in the real itself. Consequently, in Luria's myth, there is a void in the real *before*, and therefore completely independent of, language, that is, the symbolic. Further, before the articulation of the Word, there is also the divine wisdom (*Chochmah*) which suddenly appears as the image of the world, as an imaginary intuition.

Following Luria's cosmogonic myth, and interpreting its primordial moments psychoanalytically, we could put forward a logico-temporal sequence: (1) In the beginning, there was only the real (*Ein Sof*); (2) thereafter, an internal exile took place (*Tzimtzum*) (3) giving rise to a void in the real (*Khalal*) (4) after which an imaginary intuition appeared (*Chochmah*) (5) which became the model for the world that was created by the enunciation of the symbolic Word. Or, in condensed form: (1) real void; (2) imaginary intuition; (3) symbolic creation.

I will slightly reformulate and expand this triad. This is how I wish to conceptualize inner exile: a withdrawal to a primordial *real* void *outside* language and *beyond* silence, that is, completely independent and cut off from everything having to do with the symbolic *and* its absence. In the process of internal exile, the subject realizes a radical exile not only from the symbolic to an internally excluded silence, but also from the absence of the symbolic, understood as the absence of the Other – the subject retreats into a solitude within *without* the absence of the Other. In this emptiness, the subject has no name, no ego, no identity, no language, no community; he is, strictly speaking, *no one*, all alone in a not-yet-world where there is not even silence, only nothing.

In this emptiness, the word, as such, cannot be enunciated; after the original retreat, there follows, in essence, a passive process, whereby the subject cannot but await the appearance of unforeseeable imaginary intuitions, as in the famous words of Picasso: "I do not seek, I find".[8] It is not until the image has been intuited that it may be signified by a not-yet-enunciated word. In other words: after the primordial withdrawal, intuitions *may* appear where emptiness converges with darkness in the disjunction of the real and the imaginary (where darkness permeates emptiness), and after the primordial intuition in this darkness, words *may* be enunciated where darkness converges with silence in the disjunction of the imaginary and the symbolic (where silence permeates darkness) – it is not until the sudden emergence of the intuition that the void may become negatively determined in relation to the signifier. Hence, we could extend the logico-temporal scheme above, which succeeds the primordial *Tzimtzum*: (1) emptiness; (2) emptiness permeated by darkness; (3) intuition in darkness; (4) darkness permeated by silence; (5) enunciation in silence.

It should be clear by now that the first moments of creation, understood psychoanalytically as above, after the mythical void-generating internal exile in the real, regards *only* the disjunction of the imaginary and the real, that is, the region of the void where darkness and emptiness converge. It is in this region of the field of subjectivity – and in this region only – that imaginary intuitions may appear. Here, God does not create the world, but the world *arrives* to him in the imaginary; God *finds* the world.

Furthermore, I see no reason for there to be any need for these intuitions to be signified in the process of symbolic creation. This implies nothing else than the following: after having intuited the image of the world in darkness, nothing forced God to create the world symbolically through the enunciation of the signifier in silence. In other words, God may very well have chosen to stay in his inner refuge, in absolute solitude outside the world, contemplating the intuited world without ever creating it.

The Solitude of the Mystic

This seems to me to resemble a state of things that we could ascribe to a type of personality which we could describe as "mystic", understood in a way that does not significantly deviate from Wilfred Bion.[9] The mystic has access to, and resides in, a void beyond the absence of language, in the empty gap between the real and the imaginary, where he may experience *not* the unnameable, that which dwells in silence, but the *unimaginable*: the mysterious, the vertiginous, the horrifying, the sublime. In this void, *encounters* with the real take place, but at a certain distance, so that the mystic is able to intuit them without the images being destroyed by the traumatic proximity to the real, to the obliterating *Ein Sof*. These intuitions, it must be underlined, do not actually touch upon the real, as Bion seems to suggest, but are nonetheless many times felt as coming *from* it: since these intuitions arrive by "themselves", since the mystic *finds* them, he may very well understand them as real, or as emanations of the unimaginable. In other words, the religious mystic experiences these intuitions as divine revelations, or as visions given to him by God; regarding Luria's myth, we could suggestively say that God experienced the sudden flash of wisdom (*Chochmah*) as coming from God.

The mathematical mystic may very well serve as the perfect example of this, since he intuits that which is perhaps most remote from the human being's experience of the world – which is not necessarily the divine, since it lends itself to extensive anthropomorphic or animistic attributions through specular and projective mechanisms, but geometrical and numerical forms. This would enable us to understand the experiential points of reference of the philosophies of, for example, Pythagoras, Plato, Descartes, Leibniz, and Spinoza, the aesthetic theory of truth of Paul Dirac, and the mystical disposition of many extraordinary physicists, for whom theoretical physics is perceived as an interpretation of mathematics understood as eternal and real, or, better stated, as ontic.

The crucial point is that the process of creation, exemplified by Luria's myth and interpreted psychoanalytically, may very well stop after the intuition of the unimaginable – which would imply that there arises the possibility that the mystic, after his inner exile, continues to dwell in his inner emptiness and fill it with "divine" intuitions, thus enabling an imaginary world outside the symbolic world to take shape in his real void. We could speak about this process as a *subjective cosmogony*, which is only possible after the mystic has completed his inner exile.

It is not unusual for the mystic, after having retreated into his solitude within without the absence of the Other, to feel the urge to develop his subjective cosmogony by seeking a real seclusion, many times *in* (rather *with*) silence, to protect the mystic void from the symbolic order of the community. In other words, he may also go into an external exile – this was, for example, the case for Isaac Luria, who for seven years lived as a recluse and devoted himself to mystic meditations in absolute silence.

We could, in fact, even speak of a threefold process of mystic exile: first, the primordial internal exile to a void within without the absence of the Other (*Tzimtzum*); second, an actual external exile from the community, thus realizing a radical exile within *and* outside with *and* without the absence of the Other (Luria); third, a final exile *from* the inner world, or a return to the absence of the Other, that is, to silence, where the mystic, on the threshold of the symbolic, must endeavor to enunciate and transmit that which is radically beyond the unspeakable, that which revealed itself to him in the void beyond silence. Thus, in principle, I do not disagree with Bion's audacious statement – given that it is interpreted as pertaining to intuitions *of* and not *from* the unimaginable – that "So-called Scientific Laws are vulgarizations of that which the scientific mystic can achieve directly. Religious dogmata are similarly vulgarizations of that which the religious mystic can achieve directly".[10]

The second and third exiles above loosely correspond to the archetypical image of the mystic vagabond, of which the Pre-Socratic philosopher Empedocles – with whom Sigmund Freud by the end of his life seems to have identified himself[11] – may serve as a prime example. Concerning his return to the community, Empedocles wrote: "Of these I too am now one, an exile from the gods and a wanderer".[12]

The seemingly never-ending exodus of the mystic described above corresponds to a new view of that which psychoanalysis generally speaks of as symbolic creation,[13] which Lacan understands as *creatio ex nihilo* and Donald Winnicott as being linked to the capacity to be alone in the presence of the other.[14] This view deviates from Lacan's perspective on creation – since I argue that it is linked to a primordial hole in the real, which is not created by the signifier, as well as to the generally disregarded and devalued imaginary intuition – and complements, rather than contradicts, Winnicott's, since he clearly differentiates the capacity to be alone from the loneliness associated with withdrawal,[15] which would correspond to what I refer to as a solitude within without the absence of the Other. We could, thus, differentiate between "ordinary" creation in the presence of the other and "mystic" creation without the absence of the Other.

Understood in this way, the symbolic creation of the mystic is a leap from the disjunction of the real and the imaginary towards silence. It is the mystic's attempt to return to the symbolic, where he, just like the freed prisoner in Plato's allegory of the cave, often finds himself rejected, viewed as a madman, heretic, liar, charlatan, misfit, outsider, offender; these allegations may very well turn out to be completely true, but this is beside the point. In any case, the mystic must endeavor to carry with him intuitions of the unimaginable, which he found in the void where emptiness and darkness converge, into silence, where he must endure the failure of enunciating that which is not even unnameable. Hence, the oscillation between, on the one hand, *prosaic* theoretical or dogmatic constructions cut off from the void where the primordial intuition appeared and, on the other, *poetic* speech reverberating with the vividness of the intuitive images in the void beyond silence. Consequently, broadly speaking we may differentiate between two forms of mystic speech, both enunciated in silence, supplementing the inability to signify the unimaginable: the *prosaic* speech of the theoretical mystic – who for this very reason many times does not appear to be a mystic at all, as in the case of Ludwig Wittgenstein – and the *poetic* speech of the eccentric, charismatic, or esoteric mystic. Both these cases must be understood as failed attempts to return to the symbolic: the mystic is always misunderstood, even when he is understood, accepted, recognized, celebrated, or admired.

I do not believe it is the purpose or function of the community to produce a mystic.[16] I believe it is the fate of the mystic to be alone. Given that he succeeds in failing to return to the community through creation, the community, in turn, is bound to fail to perceive that he who is speaking to them is precisely *not* the creator. The mystic creator is nowhere to be found in the realm of his symbolic creations. This is the intended meaning of Arthur Rimbaud's "*Je est un autre*", "*I* is an other": he speaks of the "false meaning of the Self" only in relation to writers who are "claiming to be the authors" of their own works.[17] The creator remains elsewhere, in solitude beyond silence, accompanied by vivid intuitions of the unimaginable, and creates solely as a response to their emergence – "one must be a *seer*, make oneself a *seer*".[18] Accordingly, one could say that God, in essence, is he who suddenly witnessed the appearance of the image of the world in solitude beyond silence, and not he who is reflected back by the world which he, it may be argued, failed miserably in creating by enunciating the Word. In the light of this, "In the beginning was the Word, and the Word was with God, and the Word was God" (John 1:1) is a testament to the solitude of God, and the *Shahada*, "There is no god but God", which the community understands as a confession of faith, is perhaps but God's confession of dejection.

For why did God create the world? Because he was alone. "I was a hidden treasure", God said according to a famous *Hadith*, "and I wanted to be known, hence I created the world so that I would be known". But since God is absolute, unique, unthinkable being, and consequently, following the great Sufi Ibn Arabi (1165–1240), since everything that exists *is* God, there is nothing beside God by which he may be known. Thus, God, who is everything that exists, created the world, which is everything that is not God: pure non-existence, empty, just like a mirror – for the world is an empty mirror.[19] Everything that exists in the world is God and not God, everything that exists is God reflected in non-existence. Thus, the human being does not exist in himself, but exists only insofar as he is a mirror for God, and only insofar as his purpose is to make God know himself through his own reflection in non-existent otherness.[20] Hence, the mystic, looking inwards, sees nothing but nothing, and in this nothing, an empty mirror, and in this mirror, a reflection of the lone God who longs to be known, and in the solitude of God, he perceives himself: "He is your mirror and you are His mirror in which He contemplates ... naught other than Himself".[21] Or, in the words of Meister Eckhart, "the soul must be alone, as God is alone", for "God became another self in order that I might become another him".[22]

But the mystic will perhaps never find the remedy for his solitude in the community. He may search for a place to belong elsewhere. He may yearn for *fanā'*, the annihilation of the self, "to die before one dies", by merging with the unimaginable through ἕνωσις, through *unio mystica*, as desired the Sufi martyr Mansur Al-Hallaj (c. 858–922): "Between me and You, there is only me. Take away the me, so only You remain". Or, he may long for a friend, a fellow mystic to coalesce with, like the dervish Shams of Tabriz (1185–1248) who, while wandering around the Middle East in search of a companion, found the Sufi poet Jalal al-Din Rumi (1207–1273), who, in turn, while desperately searching for Shams after his inexplicable disappearance, suddenly came to a realization: "Why should I seek? I am the same as he. His essence speaks through me. I have been looking for myself!".[23] And let us not forget Rimbaud, who found his Verlaine, before exiling himself to far away jungles and deserts.

Yet, it is not necessary to try to imagine the mystic happy. The mystic speaks of love and joy, awe and peace, beauty and faith. The solitude to which he is bound is not only the most fundamental condition for his sadness, but also for his happiness – for he is alone with the unimaginable.[24] Perhaps he manages to remain faithful to the unimaginable while being alone amongst others in the community; perhaps he manages to be loyal to his visions, rather than his field; to God, rather than religion; to heaven, rather than earth; to beauty, rather than art; to discovery, rather than science; to truth, rather than knowledge. Perhaps giving through creating is an act of gratitude, and contributing a form of transmission. And perhaps he prefers his solitude beyond silence because it is the only place where he is not alone.

The Poetic Art of Interpretation

The clinical implications of these reflections on solitude within without the absence of the Other as a precondition for mystic intuition and symbolic creation as failed reversed exile into the absence of community are significant, especially if: (1) the psychoanalyst has mystical tendencies, in the sense of having access to an extra-symbolic space where vivid intuitions may emerge; (2) the analysand has mystical tendencies, or shares the solitude of the mystic; (3) interpretation is thought of as creation, as *ars interpretandi*. In other words, it may not be of value for everyone. It requires something of the analyst and, to a lesser degree, of the analysand which is difficult to acquire other than through the subjective destitution that accompanies the experience of enduring solitude beyond silence.[25]

The problem revolves around the fact that psychoanalysis is a talking cure. It is generally accepted that intellectualization constitutes one of the most stubborn impasses in the clinical situation, and that it is of great import that the analyst avoids it at all costs. It is especially important that the analyst has gone through his own analysis (or self-analysis) and developed a capacity to freely enter and leave his inner refuge so as to enable intuitions to appear and signify them in a symbolically created interpretation *without* his speech being of a prosaic nature, that is, intellectualized and, so to speak, "dead". The alternative, hence, is that the psychoanalyst develops his capacity for poetic interpretations, which do *not* aim at interpreting either defense mechanisms, transference, or the symbolic formations of the unconscious, but rather strive to resonate in the corresponding void of the analysand. This is of major importance when working with gifted analysands which we could describe as having features of a "schizoid" nature, that is, subjects who have withdrawn from silence into an inner world populated by animated intuitions which often tend to lose their vividness when expressed prosaically. A subset of these subjects may be assumed to have a mystical disposition without having managed to exile themselves from their inner refuge towards silence, meaning, they have not been able to use creation as a means to return to the absence of the Other. Thus, to enable this return, it is imperative that the psychoanalyst helps the analysand to create silence.

For this to be possible, the interpretation must: (1) resist being grasped prosaically, thus circumventing the pre-conscious *and* unconscious layers of language so as for the interpretation to immediately reach the more intuitive regions of the field of subjectivity, thereby enabling that which is not even unspeakable to be grasped intuitively, that is, articulate a speech which does not correspond to any particular signification which the analysand bears for its value to be determined by the analysand's intuition only, so that "dead words" and "vivid (intuited) images" may encounter in the disjunction of the symbolic and the imaginary; and (2) be enunciated by a voice that has not been wholly domesticated by language, that has not lost the musicality that characterizes poetic speech. The vividness of the intuitions *of the analyst*, which is doomed to be lost in the interpretation understood as symbolic creation, must be transmitted by the living voice for it to create a silence in the language of the analysand through which it may pass so as to reach darkness, where the lack of signification may be filled with intuitions arriving from the disjunction of the real and the imaginary. This encounter between poetic interpretation and intuitive reception, between the vivid words of the analyst and the vivid imagery of the analysand, serves to *animate* the speech of the analysand – essentially, the aim is to arrive at "the creation of poetic style [of speech] before [speech in] prose",[26] enabling another form of dialogue to commence, one which is conditioned by the intuitive seeing of *both* the analyst and the analysand, and a poetic tone which reverberates beyond the absence of language, in order to open up a path between the inner refuge and silence, between solitude within *without* the absence of the Other and solitude without *with* the absence of the Other, between solitude in a *space* beyond silence and solitude in silence understood as a void in *structure*, allowing speech to become a means for the analysand's being, which has remained bound to the images that populate his inner emptiness, to begin to approach the absence of the Other, ultimately transforming his solitude and enabling mourning, love, desire, and belonging – for poetry is the language of solitude.

This perspective on the poetic art of interpretation differs significantly from – and since it concerns a different region of the field of subjectivity, complements rather than contradicts – the one about which Jacques Lacan, in his 24th seminar, said: "It is in as much as a correct interpretation extinguishes a symptom, that the truth is specified as being poetic. ... We have nothing beautiful to say. A different resonance is at stake, one founded on the witticism".[27] While the poetic interpretation linked to the wit seeks to reach the level of the symptomatic formation, understood as "the effect of the Symbolic in the Real",[28] this form of poetic interpretation seeks to reach the disjunction of the imaginary and the real – where there are no symptoms – thus enabling the analysand to fail to transmit the intuitions that populate his inner world through symbolic creation. Thus, we may *also* say that it is in as much as the interpretation reverberates in solitude within without the absence of the Other, that the truth is specified as being poetic.[29]

Notes

1 I have chosen to interpret *Tzimtzum* as an internal exile in accordance with Gershom Scholem, *Major Trends in Jewish Mysticism* (New York: Schocken, 1941), pp. 244–251.
2 Gershom Scholem (ed.), *Zohar* (New York: Schocken, 1977), p. 51f.
3 Scholem, *Major Trends in Jewish Mysticism*, p. 261.
4 Jacques Lacan, *Seminar XI*, p. 212.
5 There is arguably no better historical example of this than that of the Jewish community, in their incessant attempts to "solve" the problems pertaining to external exile and all the internal lines of conflict of the diaspora which follows from it. In a certain sense, it could perhaps be said that a part of the specificity of the Jewish tradition could be understood as a (at times obsessional) response to the symbolic disorder that follows from external exile.
6 Jacques Lacan, *Seminar VII*, p. 213.
7 Lacan, *Seminar VII*, p. 121. "Is" instead of "are" in the translation.
8 "What is this darkness? What is it called? Its name means nothing other than a state of potential receptivity". Meister Eckhart, *Selected Writings*, trans. Oliver Davies (London: Penguin Books, 1994), p. 224.
9 Wilfred Bion, *Attention and Interpretation* (London/New York: Karnac, 2007), pp. 62–82.
10 Wilfred Bion, "The Grid", in *Two Papers: The Grid and Caesura* (London: Karnac, 2007), p. 32.
11 Sigmund Freud, "Analysis Terminable and Interminable", in *SE XXIII*, pp. 244–247.
12 Cited in G. S. Kirk, G. S., J. E. Raven, & M. Schofield, *The Presocratic Philosophers* (Cambridge: Cambridge University Press, 2013), p. 315.
13 It is crucial to underline that all creation is not symbolic, at least not essentially or primarily. Here, I dwell particularly on symbolic creation, owing to the fact that it arguably has been overemphasized in the psychoanalytic tradition, and because I am to delve into the topic of creation in the psychoanalytic situation, understood as a "talking cure".
14 Donald Winnicott, "The Capacity to be Alone (1958)", in *The Maturational Processes and the Facilitating Environment: Studies in the Theory of Emotional Development* (London: Hogarth Press, 1965).
15 Winnicott, "The Capacity to be Alone (1958)", p. 31.
16 As thought Bion, following Nietzsche. See Bion, *Attention and Interpretation*, p. 74, 111.
17 Arthur Rimbaud, "15 mai 1871, Charleville. À Paul Demeny", in *Je ne suis pas venu ici pour être heureux* (Paris: Flammarion, 2015), p. 67.
18 Rimbaud, "15 mai 1871, Charleville. À Paul Demeny", p. 67.
19 "The Real [God] first gave existence to the entire Cosmos as homogeneity without Spirit in it, being like an unpolished mirror ... Thus the Divine Order required the pure reflectivity of the mirror of the Cosmos". Muhyiddin Ibn Al-'Arabi, *The Seals of Wisdom* (Santa Barbara: Concord Grove Press, 1983), p. 32.
20 "I have two aspects: He and me, but He is not I in my I. In me is His theatre of manifestations, and we are for Him as vessels". Ibn Arabi, *The Seals of Wisdom*, p. 60.
21 Ibn Arabi, *The Seals of Wisdom*, p. 42.
22 Meister Eckhart, *Selected Writings*, p. 230, 249.
23 Cited in Coleman Barks, "On Rumi", in Jalal al-Din Rumi, *Essential Rumi*, trans. C. Barks (New Jersey: Castle Books, 1997), p. xii.
24 As Plotinus puts it, one must be "alone towards the alone instead of." Plotinus, *The Enneads*, trans. S. MacKenna (London/New York: Penguin, 1991), p. 353:

> Whoever possesses God in their being, has him in a divine manner ... God is always radiant in them; they are inwardly detached from the world and are in-formed by the loving presence of their God ... This cannot be learned by taking flight, that is by fleeing

from things and physically withdrawing to a place of solitude, but rather we must learn to maintain an inner solitude regardless of where we are or who we are with.
Meister Eckhart, *Selected Writings*, p. 10f.

It is necessary to uproot oneself. To cut down the tree and make of it a cross, and then to carry it every day. It is necessary not to be 'myself', still less to be 'ourselves'. The city gives the feeling of being at home. We must take the feeling of being at home into exile. We must be rooted in the absence of a place.
Simone Weil, *Gravity and Grace*, trans. E. Crawford & M. von der Ruhr (London/New York: Routledge, 2003), p. 39.

25 In the words of Heidegger: "*For the few – for the rare ... who are endowed with the great courage required for solitude, in order to think the nobility of being and to speak of its uniqueness*". Martin Heidegger, *Contributions to Philosophy (Of the Event)*, trans. R. Rojcewicz & D. Vallega-Neu (Bloomington: Indiana University Press, 2012), p. 11f.
26 Giambattista Vico, *New Science: Principles of the New Science Concerning the Common Nature of Nations*, trans. D. Marsh (London: Penguin, 2013), p. 188.
27 Jacques. *L'insu qui sait... Seminar XXIV. Final Sessions 1–12. 1976–1977*, trans. C. Gallagher, p. 116. http://www.lacaninireland.com/web/translations/seminars/.
28 Lacan, Jacques. *RSI*, trans. by C. Gallagher, p. 20. http://www.lacaninireland.com/web/translations/seminars/.
29 Broadly speaking, we could differentiate between prosaic interpretations producing meaning in the disjunction of the symbolic and the imaginary, poetic interpretations in the form of the wit which aim at the disjunction of the symbolic and the real, and the form of poetic interpretations which I am outlining here, which seek to reverberate in the disjunction of the imaginary and the real. Consequently, metapsychologically speaking, prosaic interpretations amount to a potential obstacle for both of these forms of poetic interpretations which, in turn, do not necessarily interfere with each other, as long as they do not significantly alter the position of the analyst.

Chapter 2

Notes on Play

I

Play occurs in a gap. In this gap, we may observe phenomena which we could call "transitional". Nevertheless, it would amount to a theoretical and clinical error to conceive of this in-between space as transitional.

Space is not a set of dimensions in which something transitions, and the fact that transitions occur does not render it transitional; neither is space, in essence, a set of dimensions in which something occurs, although events may verily occur in it. We do not need to dwell upon the immemorial question of the ontological status of space to argue, given that the "inner world" which we speak of at least intuitively or metaphorically is to be conceived as an essentially geometrical space, that space in the psychoanalytic experience is entirely conditioned by non-occurrence. In space, occurrences *take place*; but space is not that which remains when the occurrence is subtracted. Rather, non-occurrence introduces space into the field of experience as that for which time is the metric.

Think of the psychoanalytic session. The analysand responds to the silence of the analyst with silence. First, discursive space emerges as the temporal distance between two continuous series of enunciations; silence is experienced as a duration whose being is contingent on it being endured. Second, by being endured as a cut between enunciations, silence, inversely, enables enunciations to be experienced as cuts in silence, that is, as *occurrences* which may or may not take place in the very space which they gave rise to by not occurring. Hence, silence, which was initially produced as spatial temporality, as endured duration between continuous series of enunciations, becomes temporal spatiality, eternal extension in which occurrences of finite duration may or may not take place.

Ultimately, all enunciations are occurrences which may or may not take place in silence. In psychoanalysis, silence grounds itself as *the* space wherein speech takes place *qua* occurrence.

II

Even if we do affirm the essentialities of Donald Winnicott's theory of transitional phenomena, we must repudiate his conception of space as transitional. Transitional

DOI: 10.4324/9781003278740-3

phenomena take place in a space that is not transitional; the process does not determine the space. This space is just a space: an eternal extension in which occurrences of finite duration may or may not take place, and which is introduced into the field of experience by non-occurrence as that for which time is the metric. Which means nothing but the following: transitional phenomena are ultimately occurrences which may or may not take place; there are occurrences which may or may not take place that are not transitional; it may very well be the case that nothing takes place; space originally emerges as non-occurrence which is endured as time.

III

Why do transitional phenomena, such as play, take place? Because space is empty. In the mirror stage, the field of subjectivity oscillates between two fundamental states. The first state is conditioned by the presence of the other, who reflects back an integral image which the child recognizes as himself, making him forget the fact that he is but a pathetic lump of fragmented anxiety. The second state corresponds to the non-presence of the mirror image, leaving the child in a state dominated by overwhelming disorder and despair. In other words, there is an oscillation between states characterized by real and imaginary modes of "functioning", respectively; modes which, in turn, are conditioned by meta-stable primary narcissism and its dependence on the functioning of the mirror.

Since we are speaking about a "phase" which arguably occurs "before" the symbolic has been inscribed as an order in its own right, it would be erroneous to speak of the non-presence of the other as absence. Absence is a symbolic category which implies the eventuality of the transition into its opposite. We could follow André Green and distinguish between absence and loss. What, then, is a loss on the level of the mirror stage? It is the non-presence of the mirror. The child is no one, all alone. The other, a shadow which falls upon his being. The child descends into an imaginary void – darkness. But loss is also, and most importantly, a hole in the real, a "hole in existence".[1] The child is deprived of life.

So, we have a hole, and we could conceive of this hole as the *non-effects* of the real on the field of subjectivity, and we may call this hole emptiness. What takes place in this emptiness? First, and by definition, nothing. The non-effects of the real, however, make this "nothing occurs" endurable; these non-effects endure, and this endurable duration constitutes the original condition for the emergence *not* of absence, but of *distance*, and this distance, in turn, enables the constitution of a subjective disposition which we could describe as "to wait and see". For what? It is of secondary importance. It is a seeing which awaits the arrival of the distant. In other words, distance as endured duration gives rise to a *space* in which occurrences may or may not take place.

The emptiness which separates the atomized body from the consistency of the image of the body, the real from the imaginary, introduces the necessity of thinking space in accordance with the general framework of atomism. In this emptiness, encounters with distant elements occur by coincidence. Here, nothing is necessary, neither the "what", the "where", nor the "when" of the distant in the distance; hence, one of the fundamental reactions to the coincidental arrival of the distant is *surprise*. In play, further, this surprise is often accompanied by a sort of *Wiederholungzwang*; after the distant has disappeared from space, the child reproduces the return of the distant, again and again. He projects the image of the distant beyond the outer limits of space, into a distance beyond the distance to the edge of emptiness. The child projects the image into an empty space in the imaginary, into darkness, and waits and sees: what occurs in the borderland where darkness merges with emptiness?

Thus, the non-presence of the other coincides with a loss which opens up an enduring emptiness which amounts to a space in which "to wait and see" emerges as a disposition enabling the coincidental occurrence of surprising encounters which are repeated through the projection of the distant into darkness. This is the space in which transitional phenomena take place: the space where emptiness and darkness converge.

IV

Let us turn to Winnicott. Since the other is not present, the child is alone. He is not mirrored, thus he is no one. But he does not know it, since there is no mirror which can reflect his loneliness, which is as unimaginable as the mirror image of the empty mirror. Hence, he does not mind being no one. Instead, space emerges as endured duration of non-occurrence. He waits and he sees. Then, he searches:

> The searching can come only from desultory formless functioning, or perhaps from rudimentary playing, as if in a neutral zone. It is only here, in this unintegrated state of the personality, that that which we describe as creative can appear. This if reflected back, *but only if reflected back*, becomes part of the organized individual personality, and eventually this in summation makes the individual to be, to be found; and eventually enables himself or herself to postulate the existence of the self.[2]

"Desultory formless functioning": the real; being "reflected back" by the other: the imaginary; in-between, "a neutral zone": the space where emptiness and darkness converge.

Hence, the search occurs in a gap between the real and the imaginary, where the vitality which characterizes play animates the "self" of the unintegrated child by being reflected back by the cathected image of the mother, that is, by the other who is present at a distance but, essentially, who is not present in the moment when play takes place *qua* occurrence. Thus, the child is "being alone in the presence of someone";[3] while playing, the child is no one, but when he looks up towards the mother, he sees into a mirror which is precisely *not* empty. No one is never there.

Perhaps while playfully searching in space the child manages to find "himself" – but the end result of it all, "to be" and "to be found", must not be confused with the point of departure, which is not merely the searching itself, but its actual predisposition: the child waiting and seeing in space while not knowing that he is no one. Perhaps it may be the case that the child, by being alone in the presence of someone who continuously mirrors his creative activity, "can come together and exist as a unit ... as an expression of I AM, I am alive, I am myself",[4] that is, that the presence of the mirror enables a fortunate encounter between life and the ego to take place in the space where emptiness, the hole in the order of life, and darkness, the hole in the realm of "I am", converge. But, once again, why does the child play? Because he is no one. And what, according to Winnicott, is the condition for the creative activity of the human being? That the creator is periodically reminded that he is equal to himself.[5]

V

Somehow, Winnicott manages to miss one of his central points. The end conceals the beginning. The child plays because he is no one, but he can only go on playing by knowing that he is himself. He must never discover that he is no one.

Thus, Winnicott fails to perceive that there is a form of play which is conditioned *precisely* by the preservation of the ineradicable gap between the real and the imaginary, as well as it remaining unveiled by the imaginary circularity whose eventuality is immanent in the reflecting fulcrum of play. Play presumes the discontinuity between the real and the imaginary, hence the continuity of this form of play presumes the preservation of the discontinuity which ego-supported creativity conceals. It is particularly about subjects for which the space between life and image remains empty (it is empty for everyone) and open (it is not open for everyone) that we could speak of *forced sublimation* – the subject *must* create in order to not wither in darkness, in emptiness. It is a form of play in an "ego-less" space which exists although the ego was never there, a space which is generally lost during primal repression although it is not primally repressed, since it does not consist of any positive elements. There are children who play in another solitude, in a space whose limits are not determined by the oscillations or articulations of the mother and the father. There is a difference between being or not being someone for someone and being or not being no one for no one.

VI

Without the presence of the other, the child remains alone in an empty space. Nothing transitions. He waits and sees. Nothing needs to occur. Perhaps the child ceases to play. Nothing, however, forces him to do so.

I am speaking about a form of play which never ceases to take place in the space where emptiness and darkness converge, where neither the mirror nor the ego are, and which is located radically beyond everything having to do with the symbol. This is the void which I have specified as being beyond silence, and which corresponds to what I have referred to as solitude without the absence of the Other.

In any case, it may very well turn out that the child suddenly finds himself all alone in a space where nothing occurs. Think of a rift which suddenly opens up in the world. It takes a while for you to notice that you are surrounded by absolute silence. What do you do? You wait and see. Nothing happens. You look around, and no one is there. Everything is distant. Perhaps panic strikes you, for the fact is that you, without knowing it, along with the world, this great hall of mirrors, have ceased to be. Nothing moves. The buildings are still there, far away, but they do not emit any light. Yet you see them. You look up, and for the first time in your life, you see the night sky. You discover the universe. Vertigo, horror, awe.

Yes, there resides the unimaginable. It can only be found if you have not been found. "I am", and the world ceases to be.

VII

Non-occurrence is the emergence of spatial temporality; "to wait and see", its transition into temporal spatiality. At this point, everything that takes place is contingent, everything that takes place is an occurrence. There is no necessity.

This is the crucial point. You can only discover the world while being alone outside the world. It is only in this rift, between the world and the world, that it is possible to grasp the highly peculiar fact that everything occurs. The world is an occurrence.

He who is curious ceases to wait and see. He searches and finds himself.

He who discovers that everything occurs ceases to search. He is an observer, a witness, a seer. He waits and sees and remains no one.

VIII

Since "to wait and see" precedes "to search", and since the latter presupposes the existence of a space which can only come into being by enduring non-occurrence, this form of play, as it were, is more original than the one Winnicott theorized about. Its dispositional fundament is not curiosity, but awe. Broadly speaking, this distinction could be said to reflect that between the curious scientist who searches and the receptive artist who finds. A scientific discovery amounts to a triumph of the ego. The artist, on the contrary, while witnessing the arrival of the unimaginable, remains but a seer.

IX

It would perhaps not be inadequate to specify this play, this form of creative activity, where the subject discovers space as eternal extension by enduring non-occurrence, by waiting and seeing in solitude without the absence of the Other, and witnessing the unimaginable occurring far away, as essentially *melancholic*. However, it is crucial to draw some lines of demarcations within the field of applicability of the concept in question.

Freud theorized about two forms of melancholia. In "Neurosis and Psychosis", Freud wrote about melancholia as the paradigmatic example of the narcissistic neuroses – which by this point was no longer equated with psychosis – and understood this pathological condition as a result of "a conflict between the ego and the super-ego".[6] I will refer to this state as "depression", which is the most common form of depressive condition among neurotic analysands, and I will understand it as essentially conditioned by the dynamics between the symbolic and the imaginary, where the fundamental determinants of secondary narcissism are to be found, and which therefore takes place in the region of the field of subjectivity where the ego ideal is situated. In "Mourning and Melancholia", however, melancholic pathology revolves around the narcissistic identification with the lost (real) object, and thus takes place in the disjunction of the imaginary and the real, that is, on the level of primary narcissism; as mentioned above, this presumes the non-presence of the mirror, resulting in a simultaneous emergence of voids in the real and the imaginary.

Nothing, however, forces the subject to identify narcissistically with the lost object. The void may very well remain empty. As a consequence of this, we may differentiate between two forms of melancholia on the level of primary narcissism: in the first, which we could refer to as *narcissistic* melancholia, the subject reacts to the loss of the real object by identifying with it; in the second, which we could call *schizoid* melancholia, the subject does not. He waits and sees. Here, there is no contradiction between sadness and happiness. There is stillness.

Schizoid melancholia requires another solitude, without the absence of the Other, by waiting and seeing in the rift between the world and the world. It is a form of melancholia where the world may disappear completely, as in melancholic psychosis, but the world may also remain as a whole. It is wholly compatible with the neurotic structure.

Consequently, I wish to propose that melancholia – both forms included – *also* amounts to a possible variation, or substructure, of neurosis. I will formalize it as follows. In the disjunction of the symbolic and the imaginary, the ego ideal is consolidated, and in the gap around which the consolidation process revolves, the real object (*a*) emerges, in silence and in darkness, respectively, in the *hysterical* and *obsessional* variations of the neurotic structure. In the disjunction of the symbolic and the real, the phallic function is consolidated, and in the gap around which the consolidation process revolves, the image emerges in the *phobic* variation of the neurotic structure. In the disjunction of the imaginary and the real, the mirror is consolidated, and in the gap around which the consolidation process revolves, the signifier emerges in the *melancholic* variation of the neurotic structure. The empty space that remains between two orders may or may not be "supplemented" through the emergence, *qua* occurrence, of elements from the third order.

X

Superficially, melancholic play in solitude without the absence of the Other and ordinary play in the presence of the other are identical. In the very act of play, it may very well be impossible to observe any differences. If play were to be viewed as craftsmanship, we could say that these forms of play make use of the same techniques, the same tools, and the same material; they may even produce the same result. These forms of play are equal, yet they are not. Just as in the case of engineering and artistry, broadly speaking, they are different in a highly delicate way. It is very subtle. Ordinary play proceeds from that which is found while searching. Melancholic play proceeds from that which is found while waiting and seeing. The difference lies wholly in the disposition: searching or waiting, curiosity or awe, conquering or dwelling, triumphing or witnessing. For the child to not cease to play in solitude without the absence of the Other, it is necessary to not abandon the unimaginable, to continue to dwell in the space where it once occurred far beyond the reach of the reflections of the mirror. Melancholic play is a creative response to the distant appearance and disappearance of the unimaginable.

The mirror mirrors everything imaginable. Thereby, it shrouds the space which separates it from the unimaginable, the rift between the world and the world.

XI

In ordinary play, the creative search animates the ego. In melancholic play, the image of the unimaginable, which mirrors nothing, least of all the ego, is animated right from the outset. It is a vivid image with which the child cannot identify himself. It remains radically other. It arrived all by itself. He has created nothing.

In ordinary play, the presence of the mirror unites life and the ego. In melancholic play, the non-presence of the mirror unites life and the unimaginable.

In ordinary play, the child explores the proximate. In melancholic play, he shelters the distant.

In ordinary play, the child conquers the world. In melancholic play, he observes the universe.

In ordinary play, the child becomes himself. In melancholic play, he remains no one.

XII

This is the destiny of the poet. How do you speak about that which appears and disappears in the far distance? Words inevitably fail. This, however, does not imply that it is the unnameable that is at stake.

The question could be formulated as thus: what is the relation between solitude beyond silence and language? What is the relation between the unimaginable and speech? What is the relation between schizoid melancholia and the signifier?

We could preliminarily say that poetry is a melancholic play with words.

and the children play on the floor with words in silence.[7]

XIII

He who found the unimaginable while waiting and seeing has created nothing. He is but a witness:

> For *I* is an other. If the brass awakes as bugle, it is not its fault. This is evident to me: I witness the advent of my thought: I see it, I listen to it: I draw a stroke of the bow: the symphony stirs in the depths, or leaps onto the stage. If the old imbeciles had not only discovered the false meaning of the Self, we would not have to sweep away those millions of skeletons which, since time immemorial, have accumulated the products of their one-eyed intellects by claiming to be their authors![8]

The question concerns the origin of poetic enunciations. Elsewhere the word awakens. Elsewhere, it reverberates. And "elsewhere" answers. Perhaps not with words, but it is nonetheless an answer. Poetry dialogues with "elsewhere".

Perhaps "elsewhere" is the Freudian unconscious, structured like a language, the discourse of the Other. But why could it not be a space beyond silence?

It may very well be true that "*I* is an other" is but a statement about the nature of the ego. But in the light of the letter in which it appears, it seems to specifically concern the origin of poetic enunciations. The ego takes the honor for that which he has not created. The ego is elsewhere than the "elsewhere" with which no one dialogues. For the poet is no one only in so far as the non-presence of the mirror unites life and the unimaginable. He must not be, but await the occurrence in the rift between the world and the world.

> I say one must be a *seer*, make oneself a *seer*.[9]

But the mirror stands in the way. Must he therefore, in order to clear the way for seeing, tear it down, destroy the ego?

> The Poet makes himself a seer by a long, immense, and rational *derangement of all senses*. All forms of love, suffering, madness; he searches himself, he depletes all poisons in himself, preserving nothing but their quintessences. Ineffable torture where he needs all his faith, all his superhuman strength, where he becomes amongst all the great patient, the great criminal, the great accursed – and the supreme Savant – for he reaches the *unknown*! For he has cultivated his soul, already rich, more than anyone else! He reaches the *unknown*, and when, panic-stricken, he ends up losing the intelligence of his visions, he has seen them! Let him die as he tumbles through unheard of and unnameable things![10]

Perhaps this is the recipe for those who do not want to wait. Or for the analyst. It is of lesser importance. There are many ways to reach the unknown, none of which may be outlined in advance.

What matters is this: poetry begins with no one seeing the unimaginable, with visions of the unknown. Without no one, and without seeing, and without the unimaginable, and without no one seeing the unimaginable, there is no poetry.

Or rather, there is only another form of poetry, and this poetry is a poetry where the "elsewhere" with which no one dialogues is the Freudian unconscious, structured like a language, the discourse of the Other.

XIV

Yes, there is a difference between being or not being someone for someone and being or not being no one for no one, between being or not being that which one signifier represents for another signifier in language or being or not being nothing for nothing in nothing.

The poet dialogues with "elsewhere". He speaks and awaits its response. Whatever this response may be, it always reverberates beyond silence, but the response of "elsewhere" always occurs in silence – *songs without words*. The poet dialogues with reverberations in space, musically, but space responds as a hole in structure.

The eternal silence of these infinite spaces frightens me.[11]

Without knowing it, the poet has created silence, the absence of the Other – *silentium ex nihilo*. The poet creates the absence of the Other in solitude without the absence of the Other, and his solitude transforms, and a path opens up between the void beyond silence and silence in language, between loss and absence, between abandonment and lovelessness, between space and structure, between no one and not someone:

> At the time of day when the landscape is a halo of Life, ... I raised up, oh my love, in the silence of my disquiet, this strange book like the open doors to an abandoned house. ... As a weaver, I sat by the window of my life and forgot that I lived and existed, weaving sheets to shroud my tedium in chaste linens for the altars of my silence. ... And I give you this book because I know it is beautiful and useless. ... I put my whole soul into making it, but I did not think about it as I made it, for I thought only of me, who am sad, and of you, who are no one.[12]

XV

Yet it remains that the poet is no one. He is alone in a space beyond silence. He is a seer. He may enter the world and look into the mirror and see everything imaginable. He may withdraw into the rift between the world and the world and witness the appearance and disappearance of the unimaginable. In the world, he may see himself; in the rift, he may see the world – but he will never see no one.

At a certain point, the poet may begin his search of himself. He will find memories, images, reflections, mirages of himself, but he will never find the poet.

He may, however, discover that his destiny, as a poet and a seer, depends on him being no one.

I am no one, therefore I am:

> Today, I was suddenly struck by an absurd and accurate sensation. I realized, in an inner flash, that I am no one. No one, absolutely no one. In that flash, what I had supposed to be a city appeared as a desert plain; and the sinister light that showed me myself revealed no sky above. I was deprived of the power to be before the world existed. If I was reincarnated, it was without myself, without being reborn.[13]

Notes

1. Jacques Lacan, *Seminar VI*, p. 337.
2. Donald Winnicott, "Playing: Creative Activity and the Search for the Self", in *Playing and Reality* (New York/London: Routledge, 2005), p. 86.
3. Donald Winnicott, "Playing: A Theoretical Statement", in *Playing and Reality*, p. 64.
4. Winnicott, "Playing: Creative Activity and the Search for the Self", p. 76.
5. Winnicott even claims that "there is a direct development from transitional phenomena to playing, and from playing to shared playing, and from this to cultural experiences". Winnicott, "Playing: A Theoretical Statement", p. 69.
6. Sigmund Freud, "Neurosis and Psychosis", SE *XIX*, p. 152.
7. Gunnar Ekelöf, "Sent på jorden", in *Samlade dikter I* (Stockholm: Atlantis, 2016), p. 2.
8. Arthur Rimbaud, "15 mai 1871, Charleville. À Paul Demeny", in *Je ne suis pas venu ici pour être heureux* (Paris: Flammarion, 2015), p. 67.
9. Rimbaud, "15 mai 1871, Charleville. À Paul Demeny", p. 68.
10. Ibid.
11. Blaise Pascal, *Pascal's Pensées*, trans. W. F. Trotter (New York: Dutton, 1958), p. 155.
12. Fernando Pessoa, *Livro do Desassossego por Bernando Soares. Vol. I* (Lisbon: Ática, 1982), p. 246.
13. Ibid., p. 30.

Chapter 3

The End of Grief

Yes, evening will find itself in me, without me.[1]

James Joyce, *Ulysses*

Freud and Lacan

The Riddle of Mourning

Freud never put forward an explicit theory of mourning. "Mourning and Melancholia" is not about mourning. It is about melancholia. Mourning is but a point of reference serving to differentiate between the "normal" and the "pathological". As to melancholia, in order to explain it, Freud needed to first introduce narcissism as a developmental stage between auto-eroticism and object love. Before the libido clings on to the object, it is directed towards the ego, the latter thus functioning as

> a great reservoir from which the libido that is destined for objects flows out and into which it flows back from those objects. Object-libido was at first ego-libido and can be transformed back into ego-libido.[2]

Proceeding from this conception, melancholia is understood as a result of the ego, instead of letting go of the lost object, taking it into itself and identifying with it narcissistically, thus amounting to a regression of the libido from object-love to narcissism, hindering the detachment of the libido, which would enable it to freely find and cathect substitute objects. This, however, does not suffice to explain mourning as such, for even "in normal mental life (and not only in periods of mourning) we are constantly detaching our libido in this way from people or from other objects without falling ill", while at the same time "a detachment of the libido is the essential and regular mechanism of every repression".[3] In essence, the destiny of the libido is always predicated by loss – it is an inevitable factor conditioning the vicissitudes of the libido, from beginning to end. Hence, it explains everything and nothing, and the question about the affective processes peculiar to the phenomena of mourning remains unanswered. In "On Transience", written in 1915, Freud formulates it as follows:

> Mourning over the loss of something that we have loved or admired seems so natural to the layman that he regards it as self-evident. But to psychologists mourning is a great riddle, one of those phenomena which cannot themselves be explained ... Why it is that this detachment of libido from its objects should be such a painful process is a mystery to us and we have not hitherto been able to frame any hypothesis to account for it.[4]

Keep in mind that this was written after "Mourning and Melancholia". Even after having accounted for the dynamics of the libido in melancholia, Freud perceived mourning as an enigma.[5]

Freud's final words on mourning were written in 1925, in the last paragraph of the third and final section of the concluding addendum to *Inhibitions, Symptoms and Anxiety*. Here, he ceased to be bewildered by the economic process of mental pain by settling with declaring it to be a fact – "pain is thus the actual reaction to loss of object"[6] – and, further, by conceptualizing it analogically to its physical counterpart:

> When there is physical pain, a high degree of what may be termed narcissistic cathexis of the painful place occurs ... The transition from physical pain to mental pain corresponds to a change from narcissistic cathexis to object-cathexis. An object-presentation which is highly cathected by the drive plays the same role as a part of the body which is cathected by an increase of stimulus.[7]

Physical pain functions as a sort of "pseudo-drive",[8] flooding the psychic apparatus with excitations from the body, forcing the ego to act in the service of the self-preservative drive by concentrating all of its narcissistic libido to the source of pain in order to remove it, that is, to make the pain go away; in mental pain, it is the drive itself that is the cause of the unpleasurable increase in excitations streaming towards the lost object in order to retrieve it, that is, to make the pain go away. Freud appears to be satisfied with this explanation, as it enables him to occupy an astonishingly trivial view on the process of mourning as such:

> We know of yet another emotional reaction to the loss of an object [apart from anxiety and pain], and that is mourning. But we have no longer any difficulty in accounting for it. Mourning occurs under the influence of reality-testing; for the latter function demands categorically from the bereaved person that he should separate himself from the object, since it no longer exists. Mourning is entrusted with the task of carrying out this retreat from the object ... That this separation should be painful fits in with what we have just said, in view of the high and unsatisfiable cathexis of longing which is concentrated on the object by the bereaved person.[9]

In other words, Freud solves the economic mystery circularly by asserting that the loss of the desired object causes pain and that pain derives from the desire of the lost object – that loss causes pain causes desire causes pain causes desire causes pain, *ad infinitum*, until reality-testing forces love to undergo the arduous task of detaching itself from the lost object.[10] Everybody knows this to be true. After this, Freud never wrote a single word about mourning.

It is akin to hunger. Hunger is an unpleasurable sensation of accumulated excitation deriving from the absence of the object of the oral drive. This amounts to a wish to eat, given that we follow Freud's paradigmatic formulation of the pleasure principle and define "wish" as "a current ... starting from unpleasure and aiming at pleasure".[11] An excitation calling for discharge is equivalent to a wish calling for fulfillment through the presence of the object. Not eating leads to a continuous accumulation of excitation amounting to an increase in the intensity of the sensation of unpleasure. Thus, the amount of excitation flowing towards the representation of the oral object increases, intensifying the wish to eat. In other words, not eating makes you more hungry – the absence of the object of the oral drive causes unpleasure causes desire causes unpleasure causes desire causes unpleasure, *ad infinitum*, until you eat. On a purely economic level, the unpleasure of hunger and that of object-love are equivalent, and hence, if the riddle of mourning boils down to the riddle of pain, there was no riddle to begin with. The only difference consists in him replacing "unpleasure" with "pain" and asserting that loss is the cause for the latter.

There are, however, a couple of significant differences between hunger and longing. First, mourning the loss of food under the influence of reality-testing will lead to death;[12] second, the object of the oral drive tends to be quite variable in relation to the fixation of the libido which characterizes object-love, and this "fixation" must hence be regarded as the very precondition for the work of mourning; third, and perhaps most importantly, there is a difference between pain and pain. Ask a starving man and he will tell you about hunger. As to mourning, it is much more complicated. Is this not the lieu where the real enigma lies? It concerns not the economics of pain, but, more fundamentally, the specific "quality" of the sentiments accompanying grief. Regarding this, Freud writes:

> If the feeling of unpleasure which then arises has the specific character of pain (a character which cannot be more exactly described) ... we may plausibly attribute this to a factor which we have not sufficiently made use of in our explanations – the high level of cathexis and "binding" that prevails while these processes which leads to a feeling of unpleasure take place.[13]

It seems that Freud, at least hesitantly and in quotation marks, has taken a leap to the "beyond" of the pleasure principle, since the specific and enigmatic quality of the pain in grief is attributed *not* to the fixation of the libido, but to its *binding*, that is, to the fundamental operation which is ascribed to the life drive – the suffering seems to be implicitly reconceptualized in terms of the life drive, which, since every psychic impetus derives from "fusions or alloys of the two classes of drives",[14] implies that the death drive must be present in one way or another. Could we not understand the resistance to part way with the lost object as an effect of the death drive's tirelessly repeating refusal to let the libido detach from the object to which it is bound? I believe Freud would not object to this.

And thus, we have come to the point where it is possible to identify a gap in Freud's approach to mourning: what is the relation between grief and the death drive?

On Transience

It is worth contextualizing the paragraph from "On Transience" reiterated above. In this short text, Freud shares with us the anecdote where he, while strolling through the countryside with Rainer Maria Rilke and Lou Andreas-Salomé, was struck by the fact that the young poet could not find any real joy in the beauty of the surrounding landscape for the simple fact that everything beautiful was destined to perish. Somewhat triumphantly, Freud tells us: "I did dispute the pessimistic poet's view".[15] He did this by putting forward the following argument:

> Transient value is scarcity value in time. Limitation in the possibility of enjoyment raises the value of the enjoyment. ... Since the value of all this beauty ... is determined only by its significance for our own emotional lives, it has no need to survive us and is therefore independent of absolute duration.[16]

It must have been quite an awkward moment – and highly comical. Freud the scientist trying to persuade Rilke the poet about the status of the beautiful on economic grounds. It suffices to say that there was something that Freud simply did not grasp, independent of if he was right or wrong. It concerns beauty and death. This must have been obvious to his companions, but Freud did not give in:

> These considerations appeared to me incontestable; but I noticed that I had made no impression either upon the poet or upon my friend. My failure led me to infer that some powerful emotional factor was at work which was disturbing their judgement, and I believed later that I had discovered what it was. What spoilt their enjoyment of beauty must have been a revolt in their minds against mourning.[17]

Freud felt so confident that he went on and published a text about it. Is it not dazzling?

I do not wish to dwell upon Freud's problems with death. We already know about the death of his baby brother Julius, the importance of the death of his father for the development of psychoanalysis, his dread of, obsession with, and ideations on death, and, of course, the loss of his beloved daughter Sophie, a loss which, in a letter to Sándor Ferenczi from February 4, 1920, he referred to as a "deep narcissistic injury",[18] while also, in a letter to Ludwig Binswanger written April 11, 1929, trying to console him after the death of his son, wrote:

> We know that the acute sorrow we feel after such a loss will run its course, but also that we will remain inconsolable, and will never find a substitute. No matter what may come to take its place, even should it fill that place completely, it remains something else. And that is how it should be. It is the only way of perpetuating a love that we do not want to abandon.[19]

I wish only to point out one thing. In the letter to Ferenczi, he conceives of the death of his daughter on the level of the ego, while in the letter to Binswanger, he conceives of the death of the latter's son on the level of the object, in the very same way that he conceptualizes the difference between mourning and melancholia, where he asserts that the mourner has "suffered a loss in regard to an object; [while the melancholiac] points to a loss in regard to his ego".[20] Naturally, we must not construct an artificial contradiction between the narcissistic wound and the void in the place of the object, since the subject always partially identifies narcissistically with the object, lost or present – but still, where is the fundamental hole localized? It appears to me incontestable that it is on the level of the object, and therefore, even if the bereaved never lets go of the object, it cannot be conceived of as a variation of narcissistic melancholia.[21] The lost object is never introjected into the ego. It remains an object which remains lost. "And that is how it should be". The bereaved shelters the sentiment of grief, allowing the death drive to act in the service of perpetual sorrow, of love of that which cannot be mourned.

Here, we encounter the sentiment peculiar to grief in its purest form. It concerns beauty and death.

Conjuring Emptiness

Lacan did not find Freud's meditations sufficient to account for the phenomena of mourning. In his sixth seminar, he asserts:

> What does the work of mourning consist of? Not being suitably articulated, the topic remains bogged down in obscurity, which explains why we have made so little progress down the path that Freud paved for us concerning mourning and melancholia.[22]

Hence, he goes on and develops his own conception of grief. First, he declares the level on which the loss is situated: "mourning, which involves a veritable, intolerable loss to human beings, gives rise in them to a hole in the real".[23] But second, since "there is no absence in the real", "no lack in the real", "no sort of gap or crack in the real", and since "by definition, the real is full",[24] this void belongs to an order from which it is excluded *a priori*. Lacan resolves this impasse by immediately relating it to the signifier:

> This hole turns out to provide a place onto which the missing signifier is projected. What we have here is the signifier that is essential to the structure of the Other, the signifier whose absence renders the Other unable to give you your answer. ... It is essentially the phallus behind the veil. This signifier finds its place here. And at the same time it cannot find its place because this signifier cannot be articulated at the level of the Other. Owing to this ... all the images that have to do with the phenomena of mourning proliferate in its place.[25]

The symbolic internalizes the hole within itself – it appropriates it, makes of it a point of gravity around which it revolves, the very site of the desire of the Other, of the phallus, that is, its ineradicable internal lack, while all the imaginary phenomena associated with grief are conceived as effects of the impossible task of the symbolic to fill this void. Hence, the question about what is missing is relocated from the real to the symbolic, and, accordingly, the enigmatic work of mourning itself is understood as being

> carried out at the level of logos ... as a palliative for the chaos that ensues owing to the inability of all signifying elements to deal with the hole in existence that has been created by someone's death.[26]

In other words, Lacan does with the problem of mourning what the bereaved does with the loss in the work of mourning, namely, "raise[s] it to the level of its function as a missing signifier",[27] and, accordingly, the place where the fundamental lack is situated is displaced towards language: "mourning coincides with an essential gap, the major symbolic gap, the symbolic lack".[28] But what is the lost object *per se* corresponding to this symbolic lack? It is, once again, the phallus, the "thing" which the subject is forced to give up during the Oedipus complex. Et voilà – the problem of mourning finds itself subsumed under the general structure of castration:

> In short, the subject must mourn the loss of the phallus. This comes across very clearly – the *Untergang* of the Oedipus complex is played out around mourning. How can we not but relate this to the general problematic of mourning?[29]

The object that disappeared in the real reappears as absent in the place of the phallus, as the object whose very loss gives rise to the inextinguishable desire of the subject, and therefore, "at the level of deprivation", of the oxymoronic lack in the real, the subject "must situate himself in desire".[30]

What just happened? First, the subject is deprived of the object, which leaves a void in the real. Second, since no void can exist in the real, it is swallowed up by the symbolic and becomes a symbolic lack. Third, since symbolic lack corresponds to castration, the lost object is projected at the level of the phallus. Fourth, the inability of the symbolic to handle this lack gives rise to secondary imaginary phenomena in its place. Finally, mourning amounts to a process whereby the subject endeavors to approach this loss at the level of the symbol. To mourn is essentially to confront castration anew.

Lacan's conception of mourning is something of a volte-face: (1) the creation of a hole in the real sets in motion a reverse process moving from (2) symbolic lack to (3) imaginary loss to (4) real deprivation, whereby the void suddenly finds itself subordinated to castration:

> What then appears at the level of deprivation [1]? What does the subject who has been symbolically castrated become at this level [2]? Note that he has been symbolically castrated at the level of his [symbolic] position as a speaking subject, and not at the level of his being. What is involved becomes far clearer and easier to indicate once we formulate the problem in terms of mourning. ... It is at the imaginary level that something is caught up, marked, and subtracted [3]. The upshot is a really deprived subject [4].[31]

But why this conjuring of the void in the real? It is quite simple. Lacan himself asserts it: "our conceptual framework and knowledge do not allow us to locate or situate this deprivation anywhere in the real, because the real as such is defined as always full".[32] The void in the real is *so* impossible that it cannot exist even in the realm of the impossible, in the real. As such, it cannot *really* be. It can only "be" by courtesy of the signifier, in so far as language engulfs it and sustains it as a hole in the real *within* the symbolic, as an abyss populated by imaginary elements through which symbolic lack descends into the unknown.

Could we not understand Lacan's contradictory reflections on the real void in mourning as a symptom indicating the site of an unresolvable theoretical aporia? Everything that cannot exist ex-sists, by definition, except the void in the real. It and only it cannot, as such and in itself, be.

It is crucial, however, to emphasize the place that this theoretically impossible void nevertheless occupies in Lacan's later teachings. Besides from perceiving the signifier as that which represents the subject for another signifier, he adds not only that its essential function consists in it "making a hole", whereby "[the] real is hollowed out",[33] but also, and even more radical, that "the efficacy of language ... is only sustained by the function of what I've called the hole in the real",[34] implying that the symbolic is nothing but the domain of the real void, of an impossible impossibility outside within. In actuality, the field of subjectivity is understood as nothing else than

> the triplicity that results from a consistence that is assigned only on the basis of the imaginary, from a fundamental hole that emerges from the symbolic, and from an ex-sistence which belongs to the real.[35]

In other words, the hole in the real is what is most essential to the functioning of language. It is the exterior heart of the symbolic. The hole in the real is a non-negativizable void excluded within the domain of negativity, and the sole impossibility that is excluded from the realm of the impossible. It is pseudo-negative and pseudo-impossible. It belongs neither to the negative nor the impossible. Better stated: it does not belong. It is a symptom.[36]

Ghosts, Spirits, Demons

Back to the imaginary, to "an image that can affect the soul of each of every one of us – namely, the ghost".[37] Lacan declares:

> Funeral rites have a macrocosmic nature, since there is nothing that can fill the hole in the real with signifiers unless it is the totality of the signifier itself ... The entire signifying system is brought to bear on even the slightest case of mourning. This is what explains the fact that ... all kinds of phenomena occur that stem from the coming into play and operating of the power of ghosts ... in the place left unfilled by the missing signifying rite.[38]

Lacan perceives the appearance of ghosts as a consequence of the impotence of the signifying system; they are viewed upon from the domain of the signifier, as emerging and vanishing in the void in the heart of the symbolic. In so doing, Lacan deviates from Freud. In "Mourning and Melancholia", Freud is explicit about the level on which the process of mourning and melancholia take place:

> In melancholia, accordingly, several separate struggles [between love and hate] are carried out over the object ... The location of these separate struggles cannot be assigned to any other system but the *Ucs.*, the region of the memory-traces of *things* [*sachlichen Erinnerungsspuren*] (as contrasted with *word*-cathexes [*Wortbesetzungen*]). In mourning, too, the efforts to detach the libido are carried out in this same system.[39]

Freud refers to the differentiation between *Sachvorstellung* (or *Dingvorstellung*), "thing-representation", which corresponds to the imaginary object, and *Wortvorstellung*, "word-representation", which would be the signifying element. I have little doubt that Freud, in principle, would agree with Lacan's claim that the work of mourning in the last instance consists in raising the loss from the level of *Sachvorstellungen* to that of *Wortvorstellungen*, but the ghosts essentially appear in the domain of the former, and, consequently, the failure of the *Wortvorstellungen* to dispel them in the work of mourning is temporally and topically secondary to their emergence. The ghosts precede the failure to conjure them. We should not hurry to abandon their proper realm.

This is the path Freud threads in *Totem and Taboo*, where the problem of death is practically omnipresent, and where man's primitive relation to it eludes being subsumed under the general structure of totemism, understood as a primordial Oedipal structure sustaining a network of differential social categories serving to consolidate exogamy. Instead, Freud follows the comparative anthropology of his time and speaks of animism, the first world-view of the history of civilization, which he understands as a cultural disposition wherein humans

> people the world with innumerable spiritual beings both benevolent and malignant; and these spirits and demons they regard as the causes of natural phenomena and they believe that not only animals and plants but all the inanimate objects in the world are animated by them.[40]

Animism amounts to an exhaustive psychologizing of the cosmos, an all-encompassing system of thought that endows life and spirit to everything that exists in accordance with man's own psychological predicament, a consequence of him "transposing the structural conditions of his own mind into the external world"[41] through "the projection outwards of internal perceptions",[42] and, accordingly, these ubiquitous "spirits and demons ... are only projections of man's own emotional impulses".[43] It suffices to say that these projections pertain to the imaginary register, to the same region of the unconscious as the courses of events in mourning and melancholia, which implies that they occur independently of the domain of the *Wortvorstellungen*:

> It was not until a language of abstract thought had been developed, that is to say, not until the sensory residues of verbal presentations had been linked to the internal processes, that the latter themselves gradually became capable of being perceived [instead of being projected outwards].[44]

In other words, ghosts, spirits, demons originally *appear* in reality as projections of imaginary elements, as externalized reflections of images of objects, and depend solely on the reduplicative and projective capacity of the mirror, while their subsequent *disappearance* is also dependent on the operations of word-representations. Even if we agree that the work of mourning essentially consists in raising the object to the level of the absence of the Other, we are still confronted with the task of accounting for the conditions of the emergence of ghosts. Concerning this, Freud states:

> When we, no less than primitive man, project something into external reality, what is happening must surely be this: we are recognizing the existence of two states – one in which something is directly given to the senses and to consciousness (that is, is *present* to them), and alongside it another, in which the same thing is *latent* but capable of re-appearing. In short, we are recognizing the co-existence of perception and memory ... It might be said that in the last analysis the "spirit" of persons or things comes down to their capacity to be remembered and imagined after perception of them has ceased.[45]

We must differentiate between the object present before the senses and its corresponding latent memory-trace, and we could understand them as real and imaginary elements, respectively. The creation of spirits could thus be grasped as the projection of the image of the object into the place which the sense object no longer occupies. Stated differently: "the spirit of the object"[46] is thrown into the void in the real. The hole is the lieu into which the image of the disappeared is projected. Consequently, the whole *Weltanschauung* of animism may be conceived of as emerging from a fundamental emptiness populated by a multitude of reflections of lost objects. And hence "man's first theoretical achievement, the creation of spirits"[47] may be understood as an imaginary response to the confrontation with the permanent disappearance of the object in the real, and thus, ultimately, with death: "the chief starting-point of this theorizing must have been the problem of death",[48] and "the origin of the belief in souls and in demons, which is the essence of animism, goes back to the impression which is made upon men by death".[49] We feel justified to affirm the double signification of Freud's proposal that "the survivors' position in relation to the dead was what first caused primitive man to reflect".[50]

Animism and the beginning of grief are structural equivalents; we may perceive them as being one and the same – grief commences with the creation of a void in the real, with the emergence of emptiness, induced by the death of the object, but the image of the dead which the bereaved searches for is nowhere to be found, so its shadow permeates the empty, and the mirror projects its reflection therein, and reappears in the uncanny dark in the guise of a ghost, which the words conjure by raising its spirit into the unspoken, into silence, in the work of mourning. The ghosts reside in darkness, appear in silence, and vanish into emptiness.

And thus, following Freud, we may rectify Lacan's reversion of the process of grief: (1) real void; (2) imaginary ghost; (3) symbolic mourning.

The Death of Death

The Phenomenology of the Spirit

Perhaps it is the case that the word is the murder of the thing, but this does not imply that the word is the murder of emptiness. The word is not the death of death. In the emptiness of death, the dead never cease to not return, whereas in the field of language, the word never ceases to be different. Language is the perpetual return of the different. Death is the eternal non-return of the same. Stated otherwise: language is structure. Death is space.[51] Between them there is no relation.

Nevertheless, death and language do not reside in parallel worlds. Between the eternal non-return of the same and the perpetual return of the different, occurs the original emergence of the *indifferent*. Or, in temporal-arithmetic terms: between the last and the enumerated lies the first; between the One and the many lies a one.

The One is last insofar as it does not return. The many are enumerated insofar as they have already returned. A one is first insofar as it emerges *once* and at once in the space of the non-return of the One, and is indifferent insofar as it emerges as neither sameness nor difference – it simply emerges, and, in so doing, does not relate to the subject. It has no preexisting relation whatsoever to the subject. It is wholly indifferent towards the subject. It is a pure emergence without antecedent or successor.

The original emergence of the indifferent occurs in death, in the space left empty by the permanent disappearance of the object – but this is the very place where the spirit of the object is thrown in the beginning of grief. Here, they encounter. What, then, remains of the object after death? The strange unity of the same and the indifferent: the experience of encountering the spirit of the dead in the encounter with the indifferent, an encounter wherein the spirit relates to the subject through the indifferent – the phenomenology of the spirit.

The indifferent appears in death at a distance. In itself, it means nothing, it wants nothing. In relation to the existential predicament of the human being, it is what is most distant; but in the phenomenology of the spirit, it is experienced as strange *and* familiar, as a familiar stranger – for the spirit is projected into the soulless, into that which is furthest from the domain of the soul, namely, into the indifferent, which is thus entrusted with the task of bearing the spirit of the dead.

In metapsychological terminology, the indifferent is the unimaginable, that which emerges in the far away distance in the disjunction of the real and the imaginary, in the void where emptiness and darkness converge; but in historical terms, we may equate it with the shards of *nature*, insofar as man once experienced the encounter with *a* one in nature as *a* god, that is, insofar as he experienced nature, that which is most indifferent to the human being, as divine. The phenomenology of the spirit provides the experiential basis of animism, and thus, since animism and the beginning of mourning are structural equivalents, for all the enigmatic phenomena pertaining to grief which occur on a level that is separated from the sphere of influence of the operations of the signifier – the phenomena which take place in the eternal non-return of the same, in a space that never ceases to be *before* language raises the dead to the level of the absence of the Other in the work of mourning.

For it is here, in the phenomenology of the spirit, that we encounter the sentiment peculiar to grief in its purest form. It concerns beauty and death – it is a feeling which borders on the one which Freud once called *oceanic*, the "sensation of 'eternity' ",[52] of being at one with the boundless, or of being in the proximity of the unimaginable. "I cannot discover this 'oceanic' feeling in myself",[53] Freud wrote in *Civilization and Its Discontents* – and is it not precisely *this* sense of remote closeness to animated indifference, to deathbound eternity, that eluded him in his dispute with Rilke about beauty and transience? And, further, would it be unreasonable to suggest that the inaccessibility of the oceanic dimension is intimately tied to his personal and theoretical difficulties in questions of death and mourning? Three months before his passing, in a letter to Marie Bonaparte, Freud described his world as "a little island of pain floating on a sea of indifference"[54] – but what Freud perhaps never managed to grasp was the strange fact that it is precisely the indifference of the ocean that makes it oceanic, enabling it to bring itself forth in man as storm and stillness, and to carry within itself, delivering, that which we, in lack of a better word, could refer to as *the holy*.

The Function of the Sacred

Death is space, the eternal non-return of the One. Language is structure, the perpetual return of the many. In-between, occurs the original emergence of a one, which, when animated by the spirit of the dead, serves as a shelter for the holy. Thus, to be in the proximity of the holy is to draw near to the emptiness where that which never returns inhabits the indifferent, and hence, insofar as the ghost is given a sanctuary therein, death is the domicile of the gods, a pantheon of spirits enveloped in what we, the living, may experience as *the beautiful*.

Moreover, we must differentiate between the holy and the consecrated, that is, between the fundamental theistic structures of animism and religion. On the level of the holy, which pertains to the realm of the gods, to the void where emptiness and darkness converge, the spirit inhabits the indifferent; and on the level of the consecrated, which pertains to the level of religion, to the symbolic order, the ghost is conjured by raising its spirit to the absence of the Other, where the work of mourning in the last instance is carried through – but there is no necessary link between them. The holy remains holy even in the absence of rites, taboos, myths, memorials, even memories, and the consecrated remains consecrated even in the absence of the beautiful, the oceanic, the divine. Broadly speaking, we could understand the ghost as that which is neither holy nor consecrated, and refer to that which is both holy and consecrated as *the sacred*.

The graveyard is sacred owing to the fact that it grants the spirits a resting place in the unity of the many and a one, of symbols and the indifferent – of tombstones and earth, and, accordingly, if we conceive of poetry as the reverberation of the word in the sphere of the beautiful, wherein speech touches upon the holy in the emptiness of death, the epitaphs of the graveyard, taken as a network of interconnected symbols serving to unify the word and the sanctity of animated indifference, could be said to constitute one single *poem* – and, furthermore, since the space in which poetry resonates is nothing but death itself, it would follow that *every* poem is an epitaph.

In other words, the poem, insofar as it is beautiful, is the point of coalescence in death between language and the holy. The poem is sacred. The poem, being situated in language, is an acknowledgment of loss, allowing the word to embrace death, thereby creating the absence of the Other, enabling longing and mourning; but it is also, by reverberating in the sphere of the holy, a form of perpetuating the proximity to the dwelling of the gods, that is, essentially, to the sensation of eternity, of the immortality of the spirit of the dead, *not* in the signifier, in history, or in memory, but in the proper realm of eternity, namely, in death – for in death, there is no death, no loss, no desire, no memory, only the sentiment of being in the remote presence of the ocean. In other words, in death, there is only eternity; in language, there is only finitude, and hence, the poem, by simultaneously affirming finitude and drawing near to eternity, binds eternity to death – this is the function of the sacred.

Accordingly, it falls on the sacred, the poetic, the beautiful to carry through the impossible task of conjoining life and death: to mortalize the living on the level of language, to immortalize the dead on the level of the holy, and to enable transient encounters in the space where they are destined to drift apart – fleeting moments of reconciliation of life and death, of finitude and eternity, of language and gods.

In this sense, Lacan falls short in saying that "the function of the beautiful [is] to reveal to us the site of man's relationship to his own death"[55] – for this function pertains to man's relation to death as such: the death of the subject and the object, of the living and the dead, and, insofar as it binds eternity to death, of humanity as a whole and, even beyond, of the world itself. Listen to the testimony of Judge Schreber:

> [It was] the most *holy* time of my life ... I believed the whole of mankind to have perished ... There predominated in recurrent nightly visions the notion of an approaching *end of the world* ... I regarded the starry sky largely, if not wholly, extinguished ... [I] thought I was the last real human being left ... The innumerable visions I had in connection with [these ideas] were partly of a gruesome nature, partly of an indescribable sublimity. ... In one of them it was as though I were sitting in a railway carriage or in a lift driving into the depths of the earth and I recapitulated, as it were, the whole history mankind or of the earth in reverse order; in the upper regions there were still forests of leafy trees; in the nether regions it became progressively darker and blacker. When temporarily I left the vehicle, I walked as though across a large cemetery where, coming upon the place where Leipzig's inhabitants lay buried, I crossed my own wife's grave. Sitting again in the vehicle I advanced only to a point 3; point 1, which was to mark the earliest beginning of mankind, I dared not enter.[56]

Undoing Mourning

Why is it that so few point out the striking visual similarity between the oceanic feeling, the sentiment of being at one with the boundless, and the striving of Freud's death drive to undo all bindings, thereby returning to level zero, to Nirvana, to a state of minimal differentiation, just like the waves of the ocean? And, further, why is it that so few point out the evident fact that, in both of these cases, it is precisely the religious feeling that is at stake? I propose that we equate them: Nirvana *is* the oceanic; level zero *is* the real void, that is, death. Accordingly, we could affirm that the death drive strives to return to death – but not in the sense of returning to a state of "being dead", but to a state of being *in* death, that is, to annul finitude by returning to space and drawing close to eternity. Stated differently, the death drive does not aim at the inorganic, but at the indifferent, insofar as it encompasses the immortality of the spirit of the dead.

Thus, in essence, we could perceive the death drive as the pursuit to reverse the process of mourning as such. In order to return to the immortality of the spirit of the dead, the death drive must detach from the domain of the symbol, break down the links which bind the object to the signifier's imposition of finitude, thereby throwing the spirit back into the uncanny, where it, being no longer dead or alive, finds itself transformed back into a vagrant ghost; then, in order to reach eternity, the death drive must push beyond the imaginary void, arriving at death itself, the residence of the indifferent, which, in turn, by lending itself as a vessel for the spirit of the dead, immortalizes it, and, in becoming a domicile for the gods, renders itself holy. Here, the death drive brings man to the shore of the ocean, to the point beyond which there is nothing left to mourn, to the end of grief – for it is here, and only here, that it is possible to extinguish loss as such, to efface death, space, void, through the total unification with the indifferent – for in the end of grief, the ocean submerges emptiness, engulfs death, dissolves space into the boundless, thus bringing the world to an end. This is the death of death.

In other words, the death drive is nothing but the pursuit of undoing mourning: the undoing of the many in order to return to non-return, and the undoing of non-return in order to return to the One; the undoing of structure in order to return to space, and the undoing of space in order to return to the boundless; the undoing of finitude in order to return to eternity, and the undoing of eternity in order to return to the end of the world; the undoing of language in order to return to death, and the undoing of death in order to return to the death of death. The death drive strives beyond death, through death, and beyond eternity, through eternity, in order to return to the *before* of the beginning of grief, to the complete effacement of death – to return to the end of the world. The death drive, being the pursuit of the eradication of space through space, is inherently apocalyptic.[57]

The ocean does not remember. The ocean is Λήθη, forgetting, and the death drive, passing through immortal life in death, leads man to the threshold of oblivion. Here, he may endeavor to bring death to an end, but he may also halt by its shore, on the gateway to the domicile of the gods, where he, for a brief moment, before returning to the world of language and finitude, may remain in the proximity of eternity, of the holy, and endure the ephemeral stillness of life in-between death and oblivion. Yes, the end of grief is the death of death, the end of the world, but, just before the end begins, there is a pantheon of benevolent spirits....

I am not there. They are here. The dead live beyond in me, without me.

Notes

1 James Joyce, *Ulysses* (Ware: Wordsworth, 2010), p. 46.
2 Sigmund Freud, "A Difficulty in the Path of Psycho-Analysis", in *SE XVII*, p. 139.
3 Sigmund Freud, "Psycho-Analytic Notes on an Autobiographical Account of a Case of Paranoia (*Dementia Paranoides*)", in *SE XII*, p. 71.
4 Sigmund Freud, "On Transience", in *SE XIV*, p. 306.
5 Although "On Transience" (1916) was published before "Mourning and Melancholia" (1917), the former was written after the latter. More specifically, "On Transience" was finalized in November 1915 and "Mourning and Melancholia" in May 1915. See James Strachey, "Editor's Note. Trauer Und Melancholie", in Freud, *SE XIV*, p. 239; James Strachey, "Editor's Note. Vergänglichkeit", in Freud, *SE XIV*, p. 304.

6   Sigmund Freud, "Inhibitions, Symptoms and Anxiety", in *SE XX*, p. 170.
7   Freud, "Inhibitions, Symptoms and Anxiety", p. 171f. I have replaced "instinctual need" from Strachey's translation to "drive".
8   Sigmund Freud, "Repression", in *SE XIV*, p. 146. "Pseudo-instinct" in Strachey's translation.
9   Freud, "Inhibitions, Symptoms and Anxiety", p. 172.
10 Freud had already stated the latter in "Mourning and Melancholia": "Reality-testing has shown that the loved object no longer exists, and it proceeds to demand that all libido shall be withdrawn from its attachments to that object". Sigmund Freud, "Mourning and Melancholia", in *SE XIV*, p. 244.
11 Sigmund Freud, "The Interpretation of Dreams", in *SE V*, p. 508.
12 Excepting anorexia, and certain forms of melancholia, where the fixation on the object of the oral drive may be understood as accomplished through displacement.
13 Freud, "Inhibitions, Symptoms and Anxiety", p. 172.
14 Sigmund Freud, "New Introductory Lectures on Psycho-Analysis", in *SE XXII*, p. 105.
15 Freud, "On Transience", p. 305.
16 Ibid., p. 305f.
17 Ibid., p. 306.
18 Cited in Peter Gay, *Freud. A Life for Our Time* (London: Papermac, 1988), p. 393.
19 Sigmund Freud & Ludwig Binswanger, *The Sigmund Freud-Binswanger Correspondence*, trans. Arnold J. Pomerans (New York: Open Press, 2003). Freud to Binswanger April 11, 1929, p. 196.
20 Freud, "Mourning and Melancholia", p. 247.
21 At least not in Freud's sense, where melancholia could be understood either as a result of the narcissistic identification with the image of the lost object or as the upshot of a conflict between the ego and the super-ego.
22 Jacques Lacan, *Seminar VI*, p. 336.
23 Lacan, *Seminar VI*, p. 336. The translator chooses "reality" for *réel*, and puts the latter in brackets.
24 Jacques Lacan, *Seminar II*, p. 313; Jacques Lacan, *Seminar X. Anxiety*, p. 132; Jacques Lacan, *Seminar IV*, p. 211; Lacan, *Seminar VI*, p. 348.
25 Lacan, *Seminar VI*, p. 336.
26 Ibid.
27 Ibid., p. 349.
28 Ibid., p. 340.
29 Ibid., p. 345f.
30 Ibid., p. 351.
31 Ibid., p. 349. Although Lacan develops his perspective on mourning and melancholia in his tenth seminar, and particularly emphasizes the functions of and the distinction between the object *a* and its image i(*a*), he does not abandon the position that the process of mourning ultimately boils down to castration:

> We mourn … inasmuch as the object we are mourning was, without us knowing, the one that had become, the one that we had made, the support of our castration. When this comes back at us, we see ourselves for what we are, in so far as we have essentially gone back to this position of castration.
> (Lacan, *Seminar X*, p. 111).

32 Lacan, *Seminar VI*, p. 349.
33 Lacan, *Seminar XXIII*, p. 21.
34 Ibid., p. 22.
35 Ibid., p. 25.

36 For the introduction of the concept "epistemological symptom", see Pablo Lerner, "The Pleasure Principle: The Epistemological Symptom of Psychoanalysis", *European Journal of Psychoanalysis* vol 8 nr 2 (2021); Pablo Lerner, "Bortom konstansprincipen", in Pablo Lerner & Tobias Wessely (ed.), *Freud och dödsdriften* (Simrishamn: TankeKraft, 2021).
37 Lacan, *Seminar VI*, p. 336f.
38 Ibid., p. 337.
39 Freud, "Mourning and Melancholia", p. 256f.
40 Sigmund Freud, "Totem and Taboo", *SE XIII*, p. 76.
41 Freud, "Totem and Taboo", p. 91. Slightly modified translation.
42 Freud, "Totem and Taboo", p. 65.
43 Ibid., p. 92.
44 Ibid., p. 64. Or, stated in the terminology of the developmental stages of the libido: "The animistic [mirror] phase would correspond to narcissism both chronologically and in its content; the religious [Oedipal] phase would correspond to the stage of object-choice of which the characteristic is a child's attachment to his parents". Freud, "Totem and Taboo", p. 90.
45 Freud, "Totem and Taboo", p. 93f.
46 I am borrowing this precise term from Christopher Bollas's gratifying "The Spirit of the Object as the Hand of Fate", in *The Shadow of the Object: Psychoanalysis of the Unthought Known* (New York/London: Routledge, 2018).
47 Freud, "Totem and Taboo", p. 93.
48 Ibid., p. 77.
49 Ibid., p. 87.
50 Ibid., p. 93. Slightly modified translation.
51 In other worlds: the inner world *is* death.
52 Sigmund Freud, "Civilization and Its Discontents", in *SE XXI*, p. 64.
53 Freud, "Civilization and Its Discontents", p. 65. It is interesting to point out that Freud, on the one hand and as we have already seen, speaks about the quality of mental pain as "a character which cannot be more exactly described", while also, on the other hand and in a strikingly similar fashion, asserts that "I am afraid that the oceanic feeling too will defy this kind of characterization". Freud, "Civilization and Its Discontents", p. 65. Freud goes on and speaks about the oceanic feeling:

> From my own experience I could not convince myself of the primary nature of such a feeling. But this gives me no right to deny that it does in fact occur in other people. ... I have nothing to suggest which would have a decisive influence on the solution of this problem. The idea of men receiving an intimation of their connection with the world around them through an immediate feeling which is from the outset directed to that purpose sounds so strange and fits in so badly with the fabric of our psychology that one is justified in attempting to discover a psychoanalytic – that is, genetic – explanation of such a feeling.

> Freud, "Civilization and Its Discontents", p. 65. He then goes on and argues that the feeling may be understood as an effect of a fusion between the ego and the external world, which would correspond to the earliest phase of the narcissistic stage, before the intervention of secondary modification of the pleasure principle effectuated by the reality principle, which consolidates the boundaries of the ego of the adult. Thus, he distinguishes between this phenomenon, understood as an early ego-experience, and the "more sharply demarcated ego-feeling of maturity". Freud, "Civilization and Its Discontents", p. 68. As I will argue later on, the oceanic feeling is precisely *not* about the ego and its fusion with the external world.

54 Cited in Ernest Jones, *Sigmund Freud. Life and Work. Volume Three. The Last Phase 1919–1939* (London: Hogarth Press, 1957), s. 242.
55 Jacques Lacan, *Seminar VII*, p. 295.
56 Daniel Paul Schreber, *Memoirs of My Nervous Illness*, trans. Ida Macalpine & Richard A. Hunter (New York: The New York Review of Books, 2000), pp. 69–79.
57 Making reference to Isaac Luria's cosmogony, we could say that the ultimate goal of the death drive is to reverse *Tzimtzum*.

Chapter 4

On God and Gods I
Truth and Being

God, Truth, Being

In his sixth seminar, Lacan asserts: "This is the big secret of psychoanalysis, if I may say so myself. The big secret is that there is no Other of the Other".[1] The signifier is difference, negativity, a reference to another difference, and the Other, being a network of signifiers, has nothing outside of this differential interplay to refer to in order to determine the value of its constituents, and thus, by extension, of itself. In other words, in the sphere of language, something is missing: that which would enable the perpetual play of the negative to turn into an assertion of Truth. Hence, we must conclude that the Other is intrinsically incomplete, and we could conceive of this incompleteness as manifesting itself in the form of an internal void where that which could hypothetically ground it, the Other of the Other assumed to fulfill the function of the Cartesian God, is not. Accordingly, there is a differentiation between knowledge and truth, between the level of the structural overdetermination of the signifying element and the absence of ground guaranteeing the truth value of every possible articulation:

> There is nothing in the Other or signifierness that can suffice at this level of signifying articulation; there is nothing in sigifierness that can guarantee truth; there is no other guarantee of truth than the Other's good faith; and this good faith always presents itself to the subject in a problematic form. Everything that the realm of speech brings into existence for the subject continues to depend on utter and complete faith in the Other.[2]

In other words, the Other of the Other, understood as the hypothetical grounding-guaranteeing reference point of the whole signifying system, is nowhere to be found in language. Perhaps it could thus be argued that truth has abandoned knowledge, that the ground of truth, being an "elsewhere" which is not, is nowhere to be found; but for Lacan, this absent ground *is* present *as* absence *in* the domain of knowledge – an absence "inside" of what is not "outside" – thereby negatively contributing to its structural overdetermination. The fact that there is no guarantee of truth does not mean that every articulation is false – which would amount to an assertion of the truth about truth – but that the problem of truth must be reconceptualized in terms of the non-existence of the Other of the Other *as* effective absence. Thus, psychoanalytically speaking, we cannot evaluate any articulation in terms of truth without first listening to the resonance in and of its absent ground; but also, since every signifying articulation ultimately presupposes the functioning of the dimension of truth, that the very habitation of the *parlêtre* in language is indissolubly tied with questions of faith. Faith in what? In the possibility of truth being spoken by language. Accordingly, and strictly speaking, insofar as speech implies faith in the possibility of truth, nothing can be said without implicitly raising the question of the ground of truth, that is, ultimately, of the existence of the Other of the Other. In his 20th seminar, Lacan formulates it as follows:

> The Other, the Other as the locus of truth, is the only place, albeit an irreducible place, that we can give to the term "divine being," God, to call him by his name. God (*Dieu*) is the locus where, if you will allow me this wordplay, the *dieu* – the *dieur* – the *dire*, is produced. With a trifling change, the *dire* constitutes *Dieu*. And as long as things are said, the God hypothesis will persist. … It is impossible to say anything without making Him subsist in the form of the Other.[3]

Insofar as the Other is the locus of truth, it is the locus of God, whom, although he *de facto* is *there* only as the not-there *per se*, is also always-already *there* as bearer of the function of the retroactive *a priori* of speech as such. He subsists independently of his existence or non-existence. He "functions".

In other words, that there is no Other of the Other means that the Other, *qua* locus of truth, is incomplete and incoherent, which opens up a rift between knowledge and truth, which, albeit being definitive, does not imply the definitive loss of truth, but a transformation of its conditions of existence. The rift between knowledge and truth becomes the mark of truth as such. More specifically, truth manifests itself in the occurrence wherein the signifier disrupts the apparent truthfulness of knowledge. This is the truth of the psychoanalytic session, outlined by Freud in his canonical writings: the truth that reveals-conceals itself in the dream, the symptom, the lapse, the parapraxis – the truth that reveals itself in the open in the form of the error. The truth shows itself as error in the singular enunciation wherein the unconscious speaks through the subject, in spite of the subject, *as* the subject:

> In short, error is the habitual incarnation of the truth. And if we wanted to be entirely rigorous, we would say that, as long as the truth isn't entirely revealed, that is to say in all probability until the end of time, its nature will be to propagate itself in the form of error.[4]

Ultimately, we could say that the error, insofar as it manifests the incoherence of the dimension of knowledge, is, on the one hand, a consequence of the non-existence of the Other of the Other, and, on the other hand, precisely that which makes its existence, as ground-guarantee of the possibility of truth, necessary. If the Other of the Other truly existed, it would immediately make itself superfluous.

Accordingly, although we cannot know for sure if the transcendent God exists or not, and in spite of the fact that he does not exist *in* language as that which would ground it, he nevertheless necessarily exists as a structural reference point supplementing his own absence – or not, as is the case in psychosis. This supplementary reference point is, to be sure, nothing but The-Name-of-the-Father, whom, by holding the very place where he is not, could be conceived of as a symptom of his own non-existence. As Lacan puts it: "The-Name-of-the-Father, that is to say, the God who doesn't exist".[5]

Moreover, it is crucial to point out that The-Name-of-the-Father is understood not only as the effect-supplement of the incompleteness-incoherence of the Other, but also as that which sustains, produces, and secures it. How? By serving as the quasi-transcendent nodal point of the signifying system as a whole, simultaneously being a part of and subtracted from it, laying down the Law, providing the signifier a point of anchorage enabling it to repress other signifiers, thus securing the operation of the metaphoric function of the symbolic, ultimately resulting in the constitution and consolidation of the primary repressed, the nucleus of the unconscious, which draws the rest of the repressed signifiers towards it. The-Name-of-the-Father produces and consolidates the internal division of the Other, gathering its ruptures under its vigilance, thereby subordinating the problematics of incompleteness-incoherence – and hence also of truth – under the general structure of repression – or, stated otherwise, under the Oedipus complex. The central void of the symbolic, the lieu where the Other of the Other is not, is being taken into possession by its own offspring. God's birthplace is being conceptualized as a product of the rule of its placeholder. In other words, the major symbolic lack is being conceived of as castration, as a result of the intervention of the Father in the Oedipus complex, representing the mythical primordial loss of the phallus and of the total *jouissance* in the nostalgic union with the Mother. This process whereby The-Name-of-the-Father subordinates its own ultimate ground *qua* non-ground, where the ineradicable incompleteness of the Other is displaced towards castration, as the irrevocable loss of the Mother, is perfectly encapsulated by Lacan in his 23rd seminar:

> The full necessity of the human race is that there should be an Other of the Other. This is what is generally called God, but which analysis unveils as being quite simply *La femme*, The Woman.[6]

In the center of the symbolic, there is a hole corresponding to the non-existence of the Other of the Other, of God – it is the grounding non-ground of truth, the condition for the impossibility of enunciating truth as Truth, and for the possibility of the truth being enunciated only in the form of the error – but that which emerges there as its own supplement, The-Name-of-the-Father, by simultaneously barring access to that which it descends towards – the Mother – makes out of this ineffaceable hole *loss*, castration, resulting in the "ambiguity" concerning what is actually not-there – God or The Woman? Perhaps it could be said that The-Name-of-the-Father, being the supplement of the former and what bars access to the latter, by occupying the very place where none of them are, equates them: God *is* The Woman insofar as the hole which their respective non-existence leaves in the symbolic coincide. This is why the psychoanalytic truth is the truth of *desire* – the fact that truth irrupts only as error is a correlate to the non-existence of the Other of the Other *qua* God; the fact that the irruption of the error amounts to a return of the repressed is a correlate to the metaphoric function of The-Name-of-the-Father *qua* supplement of the Other of the Other *qua* God; the fact that the repressed which returns as error amounts to an enunciation of the truth of desire is a correlate to it being The-Name-of-the-Father *qua* supplement of the Other of the Other *qua* God that gives rise to the loss of the Other of the Other *qua* The Woman through castration. The questions of God, truth, and desire are intimately intertwined owing to the fact that they all pertain to the very same complex – that of the fundamental symbolic lack, of castration.

Further, what is it that comes to be when speech reveals the truth of desire in the form of the error? In his first seminar, after having outlined the general structure of truth, Lacan asserts: "you don't have to go much further to see in this a structure constitutive of the revelation of being as such".[7] Let us dwell upon that which ties together truth and being.

In the real, "that which always comes back to the same place",[8] nothing is different from what it is; "all the seats are taken",[9] there is no empty space which would enable rearrangements to take place. However:

> Words, symbols, introduce a hollow, a hole thanks to which all manner of crossings are possible. Things become interchangeable. Depending on the way one envisions it, this hole in the real is called being or nothingness. This being and this nothingness are essentially linked to the phenomenon of speech. ... [The] revelation of speech is the realization of being.[10]

In the heart of the symbolic, the signifier creates a hole in the real, without which there would be no room for the signifier to oscillate, alternate, permutate, and this hole, this nothingness, is nothing but being itself, and this being is the grounding non-ground inside-outside the symbolic, and to the region that pertains to being, to the hollow in the real in the symbolic, is thrown that which is not realized in speech, that which has been relegated to its included outside, that is, the repressed, which bears the mark of negativity which the supplement of the Other of the Other fortifies in the realm of the symbol – but being, by being a nothingness which coincides with the major lack in the heart of the symbolic, is also, given that lack is the ground of desire, nothing but the grounding non-ground of truth that grounds desire as desire for being. This is why the desire of the subject, in essence, is a *manque-à-être*, a lack of being, a want-to-be. And thus, we could say that the articulation of the signifier, by creating the non-existence of the Other of the Other *qua* God, or, otherwise stated, by creating the hollow of being, provides a place for the emergence of the error in which the truth of desire may reveal itself as the realization of the being of the subject.

The Nothing and the Negative

"Is this Heidegger?", the attentive reader may ask himself. Yes and no. There are a couple of highly significant differences between Lacan's perspective on being and truth and Heidegger's conception of ἀλήθεια, of truth as the unconcealment of the being of beings. In his first seminar, concerning the lie – which in this context should be taken as representing the "negativity" of the signifier – Lacan asserts:

> The instauration of the lie in reality is brought about by speech. And it is precisely because it introduces what isn't, that it can also introduce what is. Before speech, nothing either is or isn't. Everything is already there, no doubt, but it is only with speech that there are things which are – which are true or false, that is to say which are – and things which are not. Truth hollows out its way into the real thanks to the dimension of speech. There is neither true nor false prior to speech. ... [And] being, the very verb itself, only exists in the register of speech. Speech introduces the hollow of being into the texture of the real.[11]

Without the signifier, there would be no distance between beings and "their" being; beings would be "stuck" in themselves, in a state of existence without being. There would be nothing but the real, a collection of beings that "aren't" owing to the fact that they simply "are". In this sense, there is neither being nor truth before speech, due to there being no nothingness which would enable beings to withdraw from "themselves", conceal themselves in and amongst themselves, be different from themselves, and reveal themselves as themselves in the occurrence of truth as the unconcealment of being. In the light of this, "the word is the murder of the thing" signifies that the signifier is the creation of the "loss-of-being", of which desire is a metonymy, whereby being withdraws from beings. In other words, the signifier is the sole cause and ground of what Heidegger terms "the ontological difference", the distinction between being and beings, by introducing the nothingness which corresponds to the abandonment of beings by being, leaving behind the "abyssal ground" of being *within* language, enabling being to disappear in the distorting perpetual interplay of signifiers, and to reappear in the midst of them, and through them, in the occurrence of truth understood as the unconcealment of being. For Lacan, it is the "not" of the signifier that creates "the nothing" in the real,[12] the withdrawal of being from beings, introducing the ontological difference into the field of subjectivity, and, accordingly, the word, the murder of the thing, *is* the origin of being – *creatio ex nihilo*.

The very opposite stance is taken by Heidegger. In "What is Metaphysics?", he writes:

> The nothing is the negation of the totality of beings; it is nonbeing pure and simple. But with that we bring the nothing under the higher determination of the negative, viewing it, it seems, as the negated. However, according to the reigning and never-challenged doctrine of "logic", negation is a specific act of the intellect. ... Do the "not", negatedness, and thereby negation too represent the higher determination under which the nothing falls as a particular kind of negated matter? Is the nothing given only because the "not", i.e., negation, is given? Or is it the other way around? Are negation and the "not" given only because the nothing is given? ... We assert that the nothing is more originary than the "not" and negation. If this thesis is right, then the possibility of negation as an act of the intellect, and thereby the intellect itself, are somehow dependent upon the nothing.[13]

For Heidegger, the nothing is the ground and the precondition of negation; the "negativity" of the signifier is grounded in the "nothing" in the real. They are not equiprimordial: "the nothing is the origin of negation, not vice versa".[14] What does this mean? It means that the hole in the real is not an effect of the signifier. It is primordial, it subsists independently of language. This hole is the abandonment by being *as such*. It has no cause, no "sufficient reason", no ground in λόγος; it is itself the ground of the negative, insofar as being has already abandoned that which speech negates, that which it perceives from its own domain as endowed with existence, namely, beings. It means that being is always-already lost, that there is always-already a rift between beings and being, a distance between beings and themselves – beings were never themselves to begin with. The negative is always-already predicated by the self-estrangement of that which it speaks of. Before it starts speaking. This "before" is absolute.

Again. What does it mean that the nothing is primordial? The nothing, being the negation of the totality of beings, is, in the light of the "not" of the ontological difference, that which is found on the other side of the rift that separates beings from being: "The nothing is the 'not' of beings, and is thus being, experienced from the perspective of beings".[15] But this Hegelian being = nothingness, which Lacan, following Sartre, reiterates, is valid *only* from the point of view of beings, and *only* insofar as being is perceived as the being *of* beings, that is, insofar as being essentially is understood as *that* which has abandoned beings. From the perspective of beings, being becomes the nothing of the abandonment – the nothingness of the murder of the thing, of the word. But it is not the same thing to speak of the being *of* beings and the beings *of* being, of being as *that* which "belongs to" beings and beings as *that* which "belongs to" being – or to speak of being as *that* which "belongs to" the word and the word as *that* which "belongs to" being. The being of beings, and of words, "is" their nothing, but what becomes of this nothing if beings and words are themselves perceived as *that* which being has abandoned, that is, if we perceive this nothing from the perspective of being itself? Otherwise stated, what becomes of the hole in the real if we cease to perceive it from the perspective of the word? The immediate outcome would be the seemingly trivial – but immensely consequential – assertion, that the hole in the real *does not* essentially belong to the symbolic, but to the real, and therefore the nothing, being no longer fully appropriated by language, remains a site *for* that which pertains to being essentially, and, further, since the word can no longer be understood only as the murder of the thing, as the origin of the abandonment by being, but instead becomes *one* locus which being has abandoned, the question of the status of language must be lifted anew from the perspective of being itself: "language originates from being and therefore belongs to being".[16] And thus, the question of truth, insofar as language is conceived of as essentially belonging to being, becomes not only a question of the unconcealment of the truth of the being = nothingness = want-to-be of the subject who speaks, but *also* a question of the truth of the speaking subject's *essential belonging* to being – a leap from the being of the subject to the subject of being – insofar as we grant not only the signifier, but also being *itself* the capacity to conceal-unconceal itself *in the place* from which language originates, that is, in the hole in the real *insofar* as it essentially belongs to the real. This is what remains to be thought.

The Mystery and the Enigma

What is being? Being is not a being. Being "is" not. Being is not the real. The real is the realm of ex-sistence, of existence without being. Neither is being nonbeing, the hole in the real, other than from the perspective of beings. What, then, remains for being "to be"?

Before attempting to answer this question, we must first dwell upon the essence of truth. In "The Origin of the Work of Art", Heidegger writes:

> In the midst of beings as a whole an open place occurs. There is a clearing, a lighting. Thought of in reference to what is, to beings, this clearing is in a greater degree than are beings. This open center is therefore not surrounded by what is; rather, the lighting center itself encircles all that is, like the Nothing which we scarcely know. That which is can only be, as a being, if it stands within and stands out within what is lighted in this clearing.[17]

This clearing, this lighting nothing in the midst of all that is, is what enables beings to stand out, to appear as themselves, to unconceal themselves as what they are. Hence, truth as unconcealment presupposes the openness of the clearing wherein beings may free themselves from their immediate belonging to beings as a whole. This, Heidegger, in "The Essence of Truth", terms *freedom* – but not in a metaphysical, moral, or idealist sense; it is not the freedom of the subject. Rather, "freedom for what is opened up in an open region lets beings be the beings they are. Freedom now reveals itself as letting beings be".[18] Consequently, "freedom is the *essence* of truth itself".[19] However, in this freeing-itself of the standing-out in the lighting, beings as a whole recedes into the surrounding darkness. Hence, truth as unconcealing is simultaneously, and more originary, untruth, concealing, for the unconcealment of beings in the lighting reveals itself to originate in the originary self-concealing withdrawal of beings as a whole which lets the illuminating openness of the clearing stand out and come to be in the first place. Of this, Heidegger writes:

> What conserves letting-be in this relatedness to concealing? Nothing less than the concealing of what is concealed as a whole, of beings as such, i.e., the mystery; not a particular mystery regarding this or that, but rather the one mystery – that, in general, mystery (the concealing of what is concealed) as such holds sway.[20]

The mystery, "the proper non-essence of truth",[21] is the concealing of the self-concealment of the realm of beings in which the lighting appears. The mystery is the concealed closedness of that which, by encompassing itself, encompasses the open. Insofar as it lies at its origin, this non-essence of truth, this clearing through self-concealment, is more essential to truth than the essence of truth itself. It goes beyond that which it lets come to be, the truth of beings as unconcealment in the clearing, for "the 'non-' of the originary non-essence of truth, as un-truth, points to the still unexperienced domain of the truth of Being (not merely of beings)",[22] that is, it points to the affinity between the "non" of the mystery and the "nothing" of the abandonment by being, thereby situating self-concealing that clears at the very heart of being itself.[23] Accordingly, we may ascribe to being a fundamental *refusal* to unconceal itself, present even in the occurrence of unconcealing, given that being is granted the freedom to unconceal itself *as concealed* in the very opening which it gives rise to through self-concealing – that is, if the clearing is conceived of not solely as the open "amidst" of beings, as the clearing for unconcealment of beings, but also, and more originary, as the *clearing for self-concealment* of being itself.[24] In other words, it is nothing but being that, through self-concealing, gives rise to, and gives, that through which it gives itself, by refusing to give itself, namely, the nothing, the real void, the opening of truth.[25]

Returning to the psychoanalytic field, we may use this general structure to differentiate between two forms of essential untruth, each corresponding to two forms of occurrences of truth, wherein that which belongs to untruth unconceals itself as concealed (clearing for self-concealment) and unconcealed (clearing for unconcealment), respectively. First, insofar as the hole in the real belongs to the symbolic, the realization of the being of the subject in language through the irruption of the error, which reveals the truth of desire out in the open, presupposes a more originary concealment in the realm where it emerges, in the symbolic. That which is concealed therein as a whole, and to which the being of the subject belongs, we could call *the unconscious*; but the unconscious is *not* the order to which the mystery belongs – there is nothing mysterious about the unconscious – rather, we could speak of the concealing of what is concealed as a whole in language as *the enigma*, which unconceals itself as concealed in the form of what Freud referred to as *the rebus*, and as unconcealed in the open in *the error*.[26] Second, insofar as the hole in the real belongs to the real, we leap to the subject of being, which essentially belongs to the mystery, to the self-concealment of being in the concealing of what is concealed as a whole in the real, which unconceals itself as concealed in the form of *the mysterious*, and as unconcealed in the open in *the revelation*.

This enables us to properly situate the problematics of faith, given that we understand it as indissoluble from the problematics of concealment-incompleteness. The affirmation of the error, which presents itself as the answer to the enigma, risks leading to the forgetting of the sovereignty of the "big secret". That there is no Other of the Other means that the enigma is irreducible. The symbolic is intrinsically incomplete. The unconscious is uninterpretable. Silence is the ground of language. Belonging to the enigma, speech presupposes faith to the degree that it is essentially spoken in silence. But this is also applicable to the real. The affirmation of the revelation, which presents itself as providing the answer to the mystery, risks leading to the forgetting of the sovereignty of the corresponding "secret", as it were, of the real – that the mystery is irreducible. The real is intrinsically incomplete. Emptiness is the ground of the real. Belonging to the mystery, being presupposes faith to the degree that the real essentially occurs in emptiness.

This silence and this emptiness may be further articulated in theological terms. In the "Book of Isaiah" (45:15), we read *"Vere tu es Deus absconditus"*, "Truly you are a God who has been hiding himself". Silence and emptiness are the two faces of the hidden God. Insofar as God is understood as the Word, he belongs to the enigma. He is nowhere to be found in language. He has withdrawn, concealed himself therein, leaving a fundamental hole behind. This is the silence of God. This is the grounding non-ground of language which The-Name-of-the-Father comes to occupy – "silence reign[s] where the Father speaks the Word 'soundlessly' ".[27]

But insofar as God, in accordance with the great mystical traditions, is understood as Being,[28] the One, he belongs to the mystery. He is nowhere to be found in the real, in creation.[29] He has withdrawn, concealed himself therein, leaving a fundamental hole behind. This emptiness is *not* the silence of God, the non-existence of the Other of the Other, but the non-existence of the One, the abandonment by Being, the primordial abyss of the world within; it is not the death of God, understood in terms of symbolic murder, but the death of Great Pan, a void beyond silence in the plenitude of the "Everything" – "nature is corrupt",[30] that is, the nature of the unconscious. This emptiness has nothing to do with language, or with The-Name-of-the-Father; it does not concern the God "of the philosophers and the scholars", as Blaise Pascal emphatically puts it, but the "God of Abraham, God of Isaac, God of Jacob" – that is, the *real* God of the theophanies and the mysteries: *Deus revelatus*. In other words, this emptiness, this originary *absconditio* of the One, is the proper locus of the *revelatio* of the divine in the real in the encounter with the mysterious, as concealed, and in the revelation, as unconcealed. Otherwise stated: in the emptiness of the non-existence of the One, beyond the silence of God in the midst of the many, *a* one emerges – an encounter neither with God-the-Word nor God-the-One, but with what we could speak of as *a* god.

The Mysterious

The real occurs beyond silence, in the non-existence of the One. Remaining in the beyond of the silence of God, the mysterious surfaces, as concealed, in the direction of the image, in the disjunction of the real and the imaginary, in the space where emptiness and darkness converge. Thus, in the field of experience, the emergence of a one, of a god, assumes the form of an encounter with the unimaginable. This encounter corresponds to the experience of *awe*.[31]

Awe is a disposition bearing evidence of an encounter in a void completely outside the reach of the symbolic, an encounter in the disjunction of the real and the imaginary. In awe, the subject is overwhelmed by a feeling of *being but touched by a mysterious, ungraspable Otherness which does not reflect him*. A real void separates the subject from the effects of the encounter with the unimaginable, an object which the sphere of images and significations that he bears cannot mirror. Indeed, in many cases, the lack of emptiness in the encounter with the mysterious would have resulted in horror, trauma, annihilation. Awe is an effect of an encounter with the real through two converging voids, the one real and the other imaginary; an encounter which, due to the non-effects of emptiness, petrifies the subject in a state of non-encounter, and, due to the non-effects of darkness, in a state of *import without import*: he cannot yet discern the inapprehensible signification of the experience which in a double sense mirrors nothing. Perplexed by horrifying wonder before the unimaginable, the subject is thrown into a state of liberating, ethereal resignation, an incomparable humility, a serene yet redeeming gratitude, in the encounter with that which without annihilating him reduces him to nothingness. Awe is to be grasped as a vertiginous encounter with the unthinkable objectivity of subjective non-existence induced by an encounter in the void beyond silence with the *nihilating ex-sistence of Otherness*.

In the singular, timeless event of awe, an-Other space opens up, outside language, beyond all imprinting effects of the mirror. Awe is in essence an experience of being but tangent to a foreign dimension that suddenly becomes inscribed in the field of subjectivity. Thus, awe is to be understood as an encounter with the Other of the Other, who does not exist, but who precisely *can* ex-sist in the form of a one in the void outside, and not within, the symbolic.

There is no relation between subject and object in pure awe. The object touches, but does not relate to the subject. Hence the overwhelming feeling of mercy in the nihilating event. The object of awe is so to speak unrelentingly autoerotic, its movement stands in relation only to itself. The mysterious is an inwardly vaulted mirror, its hidden interior multiplies the ungraspable Truth converging in its absent focus, in the event of awe open before the hypnotized gaze of man who, if only for an ephemeral second, discerns the contrapuntal movement of the unfathomable force in its own indifferent closedness.

Antonio Campi's (1524–1587) mannerist masterpiece "The Mysteries of the Passion, the Resurrection and the Ascension of Christ" may serve as providing an intuitive image of the unimaginable. The mysterious, depicted in the form of an arcane luminescent orb, recalling the analogy of the sphere of Being in Parmenides' poem, emerges in the far away distance, in a heavenly region radically separated from the realm where the crucifixion of the Word is carried out in the midst of the symbolic, where Christ endures the agonizing silence of God, the absence of reply to his appeals for salvation – "My God, my God, why have you forsaken me?" (Mat 27:46). This mysterious Otherness appears not only from afar but also from an *elsewhere*; its arrival amounts to a radical rupture with reality, making the subject experience, or even discover, a distance which was always-already there – the imperceptible real void. Were it not for this emptiness, this distance in the real from the habitation of the subject in the symbolic, the unimaginable would appear not only as otherworldly sublime in its nihilating Otherness, but also as horrifying, and, taken as an artistic figuration, even as vulgar; it would not be an image of resurrection, mercy, salvation, but one of judgment, doom, apocalypse, resembling the recount of the descent of Wormwood in St John's revelation of the end of the world, of the "great star, blazing like a torch, [that] fell from the sky" (Rev 8:11). But in order for the mysterious to appear *as* mysterious, it must be depicted not solely as arriving from afar, from a locus that persists independently of the lives of humans, but also, and most importantly, as essentially self-concealing, as not revealing itself in the moment of revelation – for it is precisely owing to the bewildering strangeness of the radiant orb that the subject, petrified in a state of awe or shock, may grasp *not* the Truth of the irreducible mystery, projected into the hidden interiority of the sphere, but the simple, yet incomprehensible, truth of being itself: that what cannot possibly be nevertheless is.[32]

This is the path towards which Heidegger leads us in *Contributions to Philosophy*, where he repeatedly, and emphatically, asserts: "Beings are. Being essentially occurs".[33] In other words, being, which is not, *occurs* through beings, in the self-donating event (*Ereignis*), "the temporal-spatial simultaneity for being and beings",[34] wherein being gives itself, along with the nothing in which it occurs, through refusal, in the "giving self-withdrawal"[35] whereby it unconceals itself as self-concealing, thereby disclosing the belonging of beings, in their abandonment by being, to being. In the essential occurrence of the being, "beings no longer *are*; instead, *being* rises up towards 'beings' ",[36] thus appropriating them, making the subject experience the strangeness of that which is, and the "ungraspableness of everything simple",[37] opening up "the opening of the simplicity and greatness of beings and the originally compelled necessity of securing in beings the truth of being",[38] that is, securing the truth that that which is, including the subject, which has hitherto appeared in the light of the lighting of the abandonment by being, belongs to the self-concealing.

52 On God and Gods I: Truth and Being

Figure 4.1 Antonio Campi, *Les Mystères de la Passion, de la Résurrection et de l'Acension du Christ*, 1569, oil on canvas, 165 × 186.5 cm. Musée du Louvre, Paris.

Source: https://commons.wikimedia.org/wiki/File:F0392_Louvre_Campi_Mysteres_Passion_Christ_RF1985-2_rwk.jpg

In the essential occurrence of being, in the encounter with a god beyond the silence of God in the non-existence of the One, the subject finds himself thrown into what Heidegger refers to as the "basic disposition", consisting of shock (*Erschrecken*), restraint (*Verhaltenheit*), and awe (*Scheu*)[39]:

To be shocked is to be taken aback, i.e. back from the familiarity of customary behavior and into the openness of the pressing forth of what is self-concealing. In this openness, what was hitherto familiar shows itself as what alienates and also fetters. What is most familiar, however, and therefore most unknown, is the abandonment by being. Shock lets us be taken aback by the very fact that beings *are* (whereas, previously, beings were to us simply beings) … and that being has abandoned and withdrawn itself from all "beings" and from whatever appeared as a being. … Because in this shock it is precisely the self-concealing of being that opens up, and because beings themselves as well as the relation to them want to be preserved, this shock is joined from within by its own most proper "will", and that is what is here called *restraint*. *Restraint*: the pre-disposition of readiness for the refusal as gift. In restraint, there reigns (although one is still taken aback) a turn toward the hesitant self-withholding as the essential occurrence of being. Restraint is the *center* for shock and awe. ... Awe is the way of drawing near and remaining near to what is most remote as such. Yet the most remote, in its intimations, provided these are held fast in awe, becomes the closest and gathers up into itself all relations of being.[40]

Restraint is the center of the basic disposition, the trembling vacillation between shock and awe, between being taking aback from and drawing close to the self-donating refusal of being in the event, in the encounter with the mysterious in emptiness. Restraint is the hesitant turning-towards the open self-concealment of being, remaining in a state of undecidedness between "shock in the face of what is closest and most obtrusive, namely that beings are, and awe in the face of what is remotest, namely that in beings, and before each being, Being holds sway".[41]

Being gives itself in the event in the *site* of the truth of being, in the abyssal ground where the being, through which the event eventuates, refuses to unconceal *its* truth; instead, the event, by unconcealing itself as belonging to the mystery, amounts to nothing more, and nothing less, than an *intimating* intrusion of the truth of being, an incursion which, by throwing the subject to a state of restraint, of shock and awe, takes hold of him, *appropriates* him, makes of him a witness of the undecidable truth of the remote site of the self-concealing:

> Restraint [is] openness for the reticent nearness of the essential occurrence of being, disposing toward the most remote trembling of appropriative intimations out of the remoteness of the undecidable.[42]

The event, occurring beyond silence, does not signify – it *intimates*, vividly, in the rift between sign and site, imposing on the subject a freedom to decide whereas he is to affirm his essential belonging to the remote, to the strange yet intimate site of the intimations of the self-concealing, in awe, or to the proximate, to the familiar yet alienating domain of the sign, of the abandonment by being, in shock; as such, restraint in the face of the unimaginable enables the subject, by letting the event occur in reticent silence, to *leap* into his essential belonging to the beyond of silence, to "the time-space of the stillness of the passing by of [the] god".[43] This is restraint:

> Words do not yet come to speech at all, but it is precisely in failing us that they arrive at the first leap. This failing is the event as intimation and incursion of being. This failing us is the inceptual condition for the self-unfolding possibility of an original (poetic) naming of being. ... Restraint: creative withstanding in the abyss.[44]

Reticence, the letting-go of words in restraint, is the letting-be of the unimaginable in its proper locus, in the void beyond silence, enabling intimations, presentiments, intuitions to emerge in darkness in the encounter with the mysterious in emptiness, thereby clearing the abyssal ground for a form of creation, poetically sheltering the sentiment of awe in the face of what is self-concealing, in silence – for it is only by remaining silent that the site of truth is cleared for the event, thus granting the unimaginable the freedom to occur essentially, and thus to intrude, and thus to intimate, and thus to be intuited, and thus to be imagined, and thus to be signified, and thus to be named, and thus to be given a shelter in the poem. Thus is the event preserved, by remembering it poetically through creating proceeding from its appropriative intimations, in awe, where the poetic truth which the poem shelters belongs to the mystery insofar as this sheltering preserves the self-concealment of the essential occurrence of being in the images which the poetic word awakens,[45] thereby granting the poem the freedom not only to signify, but also to intimate, and thus to be intuited, and thus to be imagined, and thus to be signified, and thus to be named, and thus to be given a shelter in the reader, poetically.[46] The poem, and the work of art, shelters the truth of the event by itself eventuating, thereby giving rise to, and giving, that through which it gives itself, by refusing to give itself – the opening of truth.

Who is the subject of being? The one who the essential occurrence of the being renders no one, who affirms his belonging to the self-concealing, in solitude beyond silence, by creating. The subject of being is the creator, but only insofar as he is not the origin of his creation, but the one who, by remaining silent in the site of truth in the essential occurrence of being, lets it originate from the event itself, from intimations springing from the encounter with the unimaginable. Proceeding from these vivid images, which are found and not created, lucid traces, intuitions, even revelations, of the nihilating encounter with the Other of the Other, the subject of being creates.[47]

In emptiness, *encountering*; in darkness, *finding*; in silence, *creating* – encountering finding creating. This is the path of the subject of being, of no one: to remain near that which is most remote, to the site of truth where the self-concealing gives itself hesitantly, and to give back, in solitude, that which he has not created, the intimations of the unimaginable, by concealing and unconcealing the truth of that which gives itself as self-concealing in signs.

Accordingly, one should avoid reducing the essence of James Joyce's writing to the operations and materiality of the signifier, exclusively emphasizing its structural connection to the wit and its belonging to the enigma. This is certainly the case – but not solely. Joyce's works occur in the intersection of the enigma and the mystery, through the concealing-unconcealing of sign *and* site, giving to the reader the opening of truth through which the poem signifies *and* intimates[48]:

Ineluctable modality of the visible: at least that if no more, thought through my eyes. Signatures of all things I am here to read, seaspawn and seawrack, the nearing tide, that rusty boot. Snotgreen, bluesilver, rust: coloured signs. Limits of the diaphane. ... Shut your eyes and see.[49]

These signatures are not merely signifiers that signify, phonetically, in silence, there for the poet to interpret, but also self-concealing signs in site that intimate, visually, in darkness, there for the poet to divine. The poet is an augur. Listen to the words "of" Stephen Dedalus, to the dynamic interplay, and analogical affinity, between the shadow of the "me" in the alienating white field of written signs, and the remote dark site of the appropriating intimations of the unimaginable, under which no one writes in solitude:

His shadow lay over the rocks as he bent, ending. Why not endless till the farthest star? Darkly they are there behind this light, darkness shining in the brightness, delta of Cassiopeia, worlds. Me sits there with his augur's rod of ash, in borrowed sandals, by day beside a livid sea, unbeheld, in violet night walking beneath a reign of uncouth stars. I throw this ended shadow from me, manshape ineluctable, call it back. Endless, would it be mine, form of my form? Who watches me here? Who ever anywhere will read these written words? Signs on a white field.[50]

Creo and Credo

Perhaps it is but an opportune coincidence that "*yo creo*" in Spanish means both "I believe" and "I create", and that "*yo encuentro*" means both "I find" and "I encounter". In psychoanalysis, owing to the emphasis on the signifier and the prohibition of the void beyond silence, there reigns a belief in the creator: a belief that the unconscious subject is the origin of his creations. This belief is determined by, and corresponds to, a fundamental epistemological repression: *yo creo* eclipses *yo encuentro*; the belief in the creator of the sign fortifies the repression of the encountering finding of the site. Hence, the sovereignty of the signifier truncates encountering finding creating; the encounter with the unimaginable in emptiness, along with the intuitive finding in darkness, disappear, and all that remains is the *creatio ex nihilo* of the signifier. We may put forward the following formula for this repression:

$$\frac{yo\,creo}{encuentro} \cdot \frac{encuentro}{?} \to yo\,creo\left(\frac{A}{creador}\right)$$

In English:

$$\frac{I\,create}{find} \cdot \frac{encounter}{?} \to I\,believe\left(\frac{A}{creator}\right)$$

The repression of the irreducible import of imaginary intuitions under the supremacy of the signifier serves to consolidate the even more fundamental forgetting of the encounter with the unimaginable in the void beyond silence, corresponding to the belief in the unconscious subject as creator. This repression has as its real historical counterpart the monotheistic centralization of the symbolic order under the vigilance of The-Name-of-the-Father, a constitutive *relocation* of the *absence* of the divine from a void outside the symbolic, to a void within it. This is how the historical leap from polytheism to monotheism ought to be articulated psychoanalytically: not solely as an iconoclastic repression of the gods by God, but also as a substitution of the void where emptiness and darkness converge, the non-encounter with a god, for the void in the heart of the symbolic, the silence of God, as the fundamental locus where the divine is absent.

We may formulate this in terms of *Deus absconditus*: where is the hidden god? Where has he concealed himself? In silence or in emptiness? In the symbolic or in the real? In language or in creation? In scripture or in nature? Monotheism is a prosaic interiorization of *Deus absconditus*, of the absence of divinity, abandoning the poetic proximity to the gods in the occurrence of the phenomena of nature in the void beyond silence, resulting in a shift from the poetic divination of the signs of the gods in the site of truth in nature, to the prosaic interpretation of the Truth of the Word in Scripture under the legislative sovereignty of The-Name-of-the-Father, fortifying the relegation of the being of the subject to the silence of God, where the unconscious speaks the truth by answering man's prayers to God with the error.

In other words, the silence of the unnameable replaces the awe of the unimaginable, and, accordingly, God is cut off from the sphere of phenomena of the gods.[51] Nowhere is this more apparent than in the "First Book of Kings" (19:11–13), where the absence of God is "present" in the encounter with the phenomena which in the polytheistic epoch were experienced as the gods; where the presence of God in the place of the gods is mediated by the voice irrupting out of a foreboding whisper in silence:

> A great and powerful wind tore the mountains apart and shattered the rocks before the Lord, but the Lord was not in the wind. After the wind there was an earthquake, but the Lord was not in the earthquake. After the earthquake came a fire, but the Lord was not in the fire. After the fire came a gentle whisper. When Elijah heard it, he pulled his cloak over his face and went out and stood at the mouth of the cave. Then a voice [i.e. the voice of the Lord] said to him...

The presence of the gods in the event is denied, the conception of the presence of the gods in the encounter with the unimaginable in nature is eclipsed by the signifying element keeping vigil over the thunderous silence in the focus of the symbolic, an emphasis consolidating the forgetting of the imperceptible emptiness which is always-already there – the event's perpetual *non-occurrence* removing and alienating and liberating man from the nihilating *poetic* effects of shock and awe.[52]

Notes

1. Jacques Lacan, *Seminar VI*, p. 298. Extracts from the first three subchapters have been published in Pablo Lerner, "On God and Gods", *Paletten* vol 331 (2023), 34–38.
2. Lacan, *Seminar VI*, p. 395.
3. Jacques Lacan, *Seminar XX*, p. 45.
4. Jacques Lacan, *Seminar I*, p. 263.
5. Jacques Lacan, *Seminar VII*, p. 181. Slightly modified.
6. Jacques Lacan, *Seminar XXIII*, p. 108.
7. Lacan, *Seminar I*, p. 263.
8. Jacques Lacan, *Seminar XI*, p. 49.
9. Lacan, *Seminar I*, p. 271.
10. Ibid.
11. Ibid., p. 228f.
12. I am here using "the nothing" in a Heideggerian sense, and not in the sense of a form of *objet petit a*.
13. Martin Heidegger, "What is Metaphysics?", trans. David Farrell Krell, in *Pathmarks* (Cambridge: Cambridge University Press, 2009), p. 85f.
14. "The 'not' does not originate through negation; rather, negation is grounded in the 'not' that springs from the nihilation of the nothing". In Heidegger, "What is Metaphysics?", p. 92.
15. Martin Heidegger, "On the Essence of Ground", trans. William McNeill, in *Pathmarks*, p. 97.
16. Martin Heidegger, *Contributions to Philosophy (Of the Event)*, trans. R. Rojcewicz & D. Vallega-Neu (Bloomington: Indiana University Press, 2012), p. 394. In this citation, and throughout this chapter, I have replaced "beyng" with "being", primarily to avoid confusion. In *Contributions*, Heidegger predominantly writes *Seyn* (beyng) instead of *Sein* (being), the former being the old German spelling of the latter. Concerning this, Heidegger states that he "writes being as 'beyng', which is supposed to indicate that being is here no longer thought metaphysically". Heidegger, *Contributions to Philosophy*, p. 344. Further, it is of importance to point out that language, although not being equiprimordial with being, is equiprimordial with the *human* being:

    Is language given concomitantly with the human being, or the human being concomitantly with language? Or does the one become and exist through the other, so that they are not at all *two* different entities? And why? Because both *belong* equiprimordually to being.

    (Heidegger, Contributions to Philosophy, p. 393).

17. Martin Heidegger, "The Origin of the Works of Art", in *Poetry, Language, Thought*, trans. A. Hofstadter (New York: Harper, 2001), p. 51.
18. Heidegger, "On the Essence of Truth", p. 144.
19. Ibid., p. 143.
20. Ibid., p. 148.
21. Ibid.
22. Ibid., p. 149.
23. "Truth signifies sheltering that clears as the fundamental trait of Being. ... Because sheltering that clears belongs to it, Being appears originally in the light of concealing withdrawal". Heidegger, "On the Essence of Truth", 153f. I have changed "Beyng" to "Being" in the second (but not the first) occasion.
24.
    The essential occurrence of the original truth can be experienced only if this cleared 'amidst', which grounds itself and determines time-space, is reached in a leap as that

from which and for which it is the clearing, namely, for *self-concealing* ... [which] is an essential character of *being*.

(Heidegger, *Contributions to Philosophy*, p. 262).

25

What if being itself were the self-withdrawing and essentially occurred as refusal? Is the latter a nullity or, rather, the highest gift? Indeed, is it not primarily on account of *this negativity* of being itself that 'nothingness' is full of that *assigning* 'power'[?].

(Heidegger, *Contributions to Philosophy*, p. 194).

26 Every fruitful psychoanalysis, insofar as it cannot do without the question of truth, must endeavor to give rise to an openness towards untruth – an openness that the unconscious, being intrinsically incomplete, already bears within itself – in order for the enigma, the essence of untruth of the symbolic, to essentially appear as *a* question to which the error – and perhaps the interpretation – may provide *a* preliminary answer. It must not be forgotten, however, that the enigma remains irreducible, for the signifier, understood as negativity, perpetually *produces* the non-existence of the Other of the Other, which implies that the unconscious, as such, always remains uninterpretable. Thus, the "openness" of the error is only asymptotically open in relation to the rebus (as is the case with the revelation and the mysterious). Accordingly, we may perceive the enigma as indissolubly tied to Lacan's "big secret", and, parroting Heidegger, we could say that the enigma that pertains to the unconscious is not a particular enigma regarding this or that (that is, a rebus), but rather the one enigma – that, in general, the enigma (the concealing of what is concealed) as such hold sway.

27 Meister Eckhart, *Selected Writings*, trans. Oliver Davies (London: Penguin Books, 1994), p. 257. It should be quite obvious to the reader that the signification which I am lending these words runs counter to Meister Eckhart's intention.
28 Or as beyond Being, as in the Neoplatonic tradition.
29 In reference to Ibn Arabi, we could say that God is everything that exists (Being), and the world is everything that is not God (beings).
30 Blaise Pascal, *Pascal's Pensées*, trans. W. F. Trotter (New York: Dutton, 1958), p. 155.
31 The following three sections have formerly appeared in Pablo Lerner, "Beyond Silence: On the Absence of God in the Films of Ingmar Bergman", in Vanessa Sinclair (ed.), *Psychoanalytic Perspectives on the Films of Ingmar Bergman: A Freudian-Lacanian Lens* (New York/London: Routledge, 2022), which was written in 2019. My perspectives on these questions have significantly changed since then.
32 Or, in the words of Mary-Jane Rubenstein: "[awe] marvels that beings cannot be, and yet beings are, that is to say, beings *happens*. Where being cannot possibly happen". In Mary-Jane Rubenstein, *Strange Wonder. The Closure of Metaphysics and the Opening of Awe* (New York: Columbia University Press, 2008), p. 37.
33 Heidegger, *Contributions to Philosophy*, p. 26.
34 Ibid., p. 13.
35 Ibid., p. 196.
36 Ibid., p. 195.
37 Ibid., p. 19.
38 Ibid., p. 15.
39 The translators of *Contributions* have chosen "diffidence" as translation for *Scheu*, which I here, in this quote and consistently throughout this chapter, substitute for "awe".
40 Heidegger, *Contributions to Philosophy*, p. 14f.
41 Martin Heidegger, *Basic Questions of Philosophy. Selected "Problems" of "Logic"*, trans. Richard Rojcewicz & André Schuwer (Bloomington/Indianapolis: Indiana

University Press, 1994), p. 4. Here, I have changed "terror" to "shock" as translation of *Erschrecken*.
42   Heidegger, *Contributions to Philosophy*, p. 30.
43   Heidegger, *Contributions to Philosophy*, p. 327. I have chosen to not delve into Heidegger's in my opinion quite unsatisfactory conceptions *der letzte Gott*, "the last God", and *das Geviert*, "the fourfold", the unity of earth, sky, gods, and mortals, which he is to dwell upon heavily in his later thinking. It suffices to mention that my perspective on gods differs significantly from that of Heidegger.
44   Heidegger, *Contributions to Philosophy*, p. 30.
45   "The sheltering of this *occurrence* is needed to preserve the self-concealing rather than do away with it ... there must always be a preservation of self-concealment". Heidegger, *Contributions to Philosophy*, p. 308.
46   Crucially, this is also the case for the creator in the process of creating his "own" creation.
47   Here, for reasons which I believe to be fairly obvious, I am only emphasizing creation as a response to the encounter with or revelation of the self-concealing. What is determinant for the subject of being, is not creation as such, but rather *affirmation of belonging to the site of the self-concealing in the real*, that is, of that which I call the mystery. An affirmative response may very well even be *cessation* of creation, as in the case of Thomas Aquinas, who, December 6, 1273, after a mystical experience, suddenly stopped writing his *Summa Theologica*, saying "*mihi videteur ut palea*", "all that I have written seems like straw to me". What is crucial to emphatically underline is the following: just as in the case of the enigma of the unconscious, *the status of the mystery is ethical*.
48   The very same may be said to be true for several surrealist painters, perhaps most notably Salvador Dalí, where emphasis is often put on the symbolic elements of his work, that is, on their affinity to the enigma. While not being inaccurate, this certainly remains insufficient. It is almost impossible to fail to notice the great importance of the "portrayal" of space, or, rather, the way he succeeds to open up a strange, vast site for the distant occurrence of the mysterious, of what we, in reference to Heidegger, could conceive of as the event, of the great stillness of passing by of the god. Just as in the case of Joyce, Dalí's work may be adequately situated in the intersection of the enigma and the mystery.
49   James Joyce, *Ulysses* (Ware: Wordsworth, 2010), p. 34.
50   Joyce, *Ulysses*, p. 44.
51   The following three sections originally appeared in Lerner, "Beyond Silence: On the Absence of God in the Films of Ingmar Bergman".
52   In the light of this, it could be argued that Kant's meditations on the sublime in *Critique of Judgement* falls under the category of monotheistic apologetics, owing to the complete relocation of the sublime from the precipitating object of nature to the judging mind of the subject, reflecting the affirmation that there is nothing truly sublime or divine to be found in the world, but only in the supersensible realm of reason, freedom, morality, and God. More specifically, in the encounter with the unimaginable might and greatness of nature, which reduces the subject to nothing, man comes to feel his elevation over nature due to him being able to think supersensible ideas of reason, for in relation to the rational idea of infinity, all sensible greatness sinks into insignificance, and since not even the greatest of natural forces may subdue him, he becomes conscious of his own freedom, which is subordinated to morality only, and since morality, according to Kant, presupposes God, the encounter with the sublime ultimately enables him to "recognize the existence in himself of a sublimity of disposition consonant with the divine will", and, thus, "a feeling for the sublime in nature is hardly thinkable unless in

association with a disposition of mind resembling the moral". Immanuel Kant, *Critique of Judgement*, trans. James Creed Meredith (Oxford/New York: Oxford University Press, 2008), pp. 94, 99. Now, is it by mere chance that Kant, in his major work on aesthetics and art, says almost nothing about the creative process as such, but settles with a blind belief in the creator, in the inborn creative capacity of the genius, whose natural endowment, and not his intuitive proximity to the sublimity of the object, is seen as the true origin of creation? Whatever may be the case, in Kant's third critique we encounter all the essential elements of both sides of the equation of the truncation of encountering finding creating.

Chapter 5

On God and Gods II
Spinoza, Author of the *Ethics*

The essence of untruth goes beyond language. The essence of untruth, and thus also of faith, depends on self-concealment, the origin of incompleteness-incoherence, which, by giving rise to the opening of truth, binds truth to the occurrence, meaning that truth, in the event of unconcealment, reveals itself as belonging to the enigma or the mystery, and hence, the problematics of truth – and those of being, gods, and creation, which are one and the same – is not, in essence, subordinated to language, but rather irreducibly linked to what could be described as *disruptive strangeness*. We have already spoken of the mystery and the mysterious; to conclude, it remains to speak of revelations.

In the lecture "A Note on Eternity, Time, and the Concept" in his *Introduction to the Reading of Hegel*, Alexandre Kojève comments on Spinoza's *Ethics*. He asserts:

> The *Ethics* is made in accordance with a method of which an account *cannot* be given in *human* language. For the *Ethics* explains everything, except the possibility for a man living in time to write it. ... The *Ethics* proves the impossibility of its own appearance at *any* moment of time whatsoever. In short, the *Ethics* could have been written, *if it is true*, only by God himself ... [Spinoza] *must* be God from all eternity in order to be able to write or think his *Ethics*. ... And this, obviously, is the height of absurdity: to take Spinoza seriously is actually to be – or to become – mad.[1]

Kojève is perfectly right in claiming that Spinoza, according to the *Ethics*, must have been God from all eternity in order to write the *Ethics*, but this does not imply that the *Ethics* disproves the possibility of it being written by Spinoza; on the contrary, the *Ethics* does, in fact, provide an explanation for the conditions under which it could come to exist in time, and this account of the possibility of the writing of the *Ethics* is arguably one of the most pivotal ideas put forward in the book as a whole, as it is the principal reason why the *Ethics*, which is not always read as a book on ethics, is called the *Ethics*, as well as the adamant ground, it could be argued, of Spinoza's decision to call the unique, eternal, infinite substance God, and not only Nature.

DOI: 10.4324/9781003278740-6

The problem concerns the acquisition of knowledge. For how can God, *or* Nature, be known by Spinoza, the finite human being, who, since "whatever is, is in God, and nothing can be or be conceived without God"[2] (1P15), is nothing but a finite mode of God amongst an infinite number of finite modes which, taken as a whole, and conceived through the infinite attribute of extension, constitute the material world as such, which, in turn, conceived through the infinite attribute of thought, is the infinite idea which God has of himself, and from whose essence follows the essences of all things, including that of the finite mode Spinoza, and that of the *Ethics* which he thinks? In other words, how can a finite mode of the infinite know the infinite from the perspective of the infinite, *sub specie aeternitatis*?

It is a question of essence and causality. God's infinite and eternal essence, which is the cause of all finite essences, includes necessary existence, but this is not the case for the finite essences themselves; only the essences of finite modes are eternal, while their actual existence is caused by God indirectly, through an infinite causal chain of reciprocally interacting finite modes of God in God on God. Thus, there is a causal gap in God,[3] for all finite modes may be conceived of as caused by God in two *distinct* ways: in terms of their essences, they are caused by God's eternal essence; and in terms of actual existence, they are caused by other actually existing finite modes of God.[4]

Naturally, this applies to every finite thought which any finite human may form in his finite mind, for insofar as a singular thought is conceived of as a finite mode of God, it may be understood in terms of either actual existence or essence, that is, from the perspective of other singular thoughts or *sub specie aeternitatis*. A series of connected and ordered finite modes conceived through the attribute of thought, Spinoza terms *ratio*, reason, or knowledge of the second kind – knowledge of the first kind being opinion or imagination, which consists of representations of singular things acquired through sensation, perception, experience, recollection – but since reason is only a finite sum of interconnected finite thoughts that proceeds from "common notions and adequate ideas of the properties of things"[5] (IIP40S2), it remains bound to the causality of actually existing finite modes, meaning, that it cannot possibly traverse the causal gap "upwards", abandoning the level of general properties of things in order to reach their singular essences in God. In other words, every thought that reason thinks remains separated from the eternity of its own essence.

The problem now appears clearly. The *Ethics* is written in the language of reason, purified and drawn to the extreme. It is a geometrical presentation of a collection of definitions, axioms, postulates, corollaries, and proofs, whereby eternal truths are derived from the idea of the infinite and eternal essence of God – but the language in which it is written cannot go beyond its own boundaries, meaning, that it remains on *this* side of the causal gap, and, although it logically proceeds from the idea of the infinite, that it cannot perceive it other than from the perspective of the language of interconnected finite modes. This is the paradox of the existence of the *Ethics*. It is written in a language which, on the one hand, and owing to its geometrical form, appears, and claims, to be under the species of eternity, but, on the other hand, and by definition, cannot but reproduce the distance from its ultimate cause, namely, the eternal essence of God.

Consequently, we must either conclude that the *Ethics* disproves its own existence in time, or maintain that it is remarkably *deceptive*, in the sense that it could be said to methodologically and stylistically *simulate* the eternity from which its existence is causally separated. And given that the latter is the case, we are forced to assume that there is a gap between the levels of the *writing* of the *Ethics* and the *acquisition* of the eternal knowledge of God which is presented therein in the language of reason, that is, that there is another kind of knowledge which corresponds to the other form of causality, implying that the appearance of a thought in the mind of a finite individual is *not* caused by another actually existing finite mode, but flows immediately from the infinite essence of God, enabling the eternal essences of singular things to be grasped from the perspective of God himself.

This is precisely what Spinoza describes in the *Ethics*. For there is a third kind of knowledge, *scientia intuitiva*, intuitive knowledge, which "proceeds from an adequate idea of the formal essence of certain attributes of God to the adequate knowledge of the essence of things"[6] (IIP40S2), meaning, that the finite mode is known on the level of eternal essence, without any reference to or need of any rules or order of reason or actual existence; the knowledge is not caused into existence by another thought, but emerges directly from the essence of God himself, "in one glance",[7] without delay, resulting in the unmediated knowing of the eternal essence of the thing itself. Spinoza writes:

> I thought this worth the trouble of noting here ... how much the knowledge of singular things I have called intuitive, *or* knowledge of the third kind, can accomplish, and how much more powerful it is than the universal knowledge I have called knowledge of the second kind. For although I have shown generally ... that all things (and consequently the human mind also) depend on God both for their essence and their existence, nevertheless, that demonstration, though legitimate and put beyond all chance of doubt, still does not affect our mind as much as when this is inferred from the very essence of any singular thing which we say depends on God (VP36S).[8]

But *what* is it that the third kind of knowledge can think so powerfully, and which it can infer immediately without the aid of reason, and which underlines the eternal knowledge of God of the *Ethics* on the level of essence, independent of all actual existence? It is very simple, even trivial. In a certain sense, it cannot possibly be otherwise. This is the fundamental revelation which only knowledge of the third kind may provide,[9] and which cannot come into actual existence in the mind of the thinker other than in the blink of an eye: *"God is everything*, and hence, insofar as I exist, I am not, but *God is me*; and insofar as I think, I do not think, but *God thinks through himself in me*; and insofar as I think of a thing, the thing is not, but *God thinks himself through himself in me"*.

Hence, it could be argued that the *Ethics* provides a valid reason for how it could come to existence in time, for we may hypothesize that Spinoza, who avowedly knew God through both reason and intuition, actually *saw*, in a flash, how God thought himself through himself in him, and that God's self-knowledge through him was the cause of the eternal essence and finite existence of himself and of everything which he could think of in the world, and thus, in extension, that the world itself was nothing but the infinite intellect of God thinking the infinite idea of God through God's infinite attribute of thought conceived under God's infinite attribute of extension – and, last of all, proceeding from this revelation, Spinoza wrote the *Ethics* in the language of reason in order to prove what he already knew by *scientia intuitiva*.

Now, it seems that the acquisition of intuitive knowledge filled Spinoza with joy, for of this joy speaks the fifth book of the *Ethics*, as the highest possible virtue attainable by mankind. Intuitive knowledge lies at the core of the ethics of the *Ethics*. He writes:

> From this kind of knowledge there arises the greatest satisfaction of mind there can be, that is, joy; this joy is accompanied by the idea of oneself, and consequently it is also accompanied by the idea of God, as its cause (VP32D).[10]

To know a thing through the third kind of knowledge is, ultimately, to know that God knows himself through himself in oneself *sub specie aeternitatis*, and to know that God is all things, and has been all things, including oneself, from all eternity – and this revelation of the eternal divine nature of oneself and of the world elicits a joy which, since God is the cause of everything, is conceived of as caused by God, thus giving rise to an intellectual love of God, *amor Dei intellectualis*, which, in turn, since God is everything, cannot be anything else than God's love towards himself, meaning, that "the mind's intellectual love of God is the very love of God by which God loves himself"[11] (VP35). This intellectual love of God is what Spinoza ultimately professes. It is the culmination of the *Ethics*, the path towards the highest of all virtues, *beatitudo*: "blessedness consists in love of God, a love which arises from the third kind of knowledge"[12] (VP42D).

Thus, we are prepared to propose a solution to Kojève's problem: Spinoza wrote the *Ethics* in the language of reason, proceeding from an intuitive knowledge of God, out of intellectual love of God, and in so doing he felt eternally blessed.

Is this madness? Perhaps, but it is of secondary importance. It is γνῶσις, the fundamental revelation of mystical pantheism (or panentheism), developed theoretically in the language of purified reason, elevated to the status of universal ethics, and hence we may very well argue that this hypothetical revelation of Spinoza is, in fact, the same as that of the al-Hallaj, but written prosaically in a state of inner peace, and not exclaimed in a state of ecstasy: "I am The Truth!", al-Hallaj cried out, and in so doing he spoke the truth of his revelation, but the truth that revealed itself to him was not that he was God, but that God, being everything, was him, for everything in him was God, and thus he knew that he was no one, and thus he did not say that he was The Truth, but The Truth spoke the truth of the being of no one through no one, at the cost of his life.[13]

The very same problem may verily be raised about Ludwig Wittgenstein. How could he possibly have written *Tractatus Logico-Philosophicus*, which is presented in a language that is even less human than that of the *Ethics*, and where the world, which is everything that is the case, is also perceived *sub specie aeternitatis*, as a sum of "unassailable and definitive"[14] propositional truths without proofs or arguments? In the concluding part of the *Tractatus*, Wittgenstein reveals himself to be a close reader of the writer from whom he borrowed the title of his work, namely, Spinoza: "The contemplation of the world *sub specie aeterni* is its contemplation as a limited whole. The feeling of the world as a limited whole is the mystical feeling".[15] We may suggest the same solution as in the case of the writing of the *Ethics*. To put it bluntly: before writing the *Tractatus*, Wittgenstein *saw* the world – and we may ask ourselves if he did not also see that Spinoza must have seen it too, meaning, that he saw that Spinoza, just like himself, was a prosaic mystic.

It is time to return to the field of psychoanalysis. How to understand the conditions of the writing of the *Ethics*? We may interpret Spinoza's God as the real, and the finite sum of the causally interconnected finite modes conceived under the attribute of thought as the symbolic. The causal gap in-between, in turn, we could understand as emptiness, as the non-effects of the real, of God-the-One, without which there would be no room for the form of causality which we, following Jacques-Alain Miller and Louis Althusser, could refer to as *metonymic*, owing to there being no immediate cause for its operations and the value of its elements, implying, in essence, that it is absolutely conditioned by that which, conceived under the attribute of thought, from the perspective of the symbolic, manifests itself as the silence of God. On the other hand, the pantheistic revelation – which irrupts in the disjunction of the real and the imaginary – wherein the subject sees the that God sees himself through himself in him, reveals that God, in the guise of the unimaginable, is hidden in plain sight *everywhere*, and, in so being, is absolutely manifest everywhere as *everything*, thereby revealing for the subject that his own existence is nothing but a manifestation of the self-concealing, and, thus, that he, owing to the simple fact that he exists, belongs to God, to the world, to being, to the real, to the mystery.

These two levels – which pertain to the enigma and the mystery, respectively – are topically separated. The writing of the *Ethics* evidently takes place on the level of the symbolic, but the acquisition of the knowledge which he develops therein appears to have emerged in the void beyond silence in the form of a revelation. What would thus be particularly deceptive about the *Ethics* is that it could be conceived of as assuming the form of a rebus which Spinoza created for himself in order to solve it in the language of reason proceeding from a solution which revealed itself to him in the form of an intuition *before* he even started writing it.[16] If this is indeed the case, then we may truly ask ourselves if the *Ethics* would, or even could, have ever been written by Spinoza were it not for the emergence of this appropriating intuition, which revealed to him his essential belonging to the domain of the unimaginable, and, furthermore, if it were not for him affirming this revelation as essentially *true*.

The pivotal point is that the revelation is *causative*. Given that we hold on to Lacan's conception of truth as cause, it is necessary to point out that revelations and intuitions have served, and will continue to serve, as precipitating causes for the creation of an uncountable number of epochal works of art, literature, philosophy, science, and religion.[17] Should not this, in combination with its structural affinity to the error, oblige us to at least consider ascribing the revelation a truth value, instead of simply declaring it to be a mere illusion, mirage, specter? All that is required is that we cease to insist that intuitions should be conceived from the perspective of the symbolic, and, moreover, that we detach the concept of truth from language, and instead tie it to the general problematics of untruth, that is, to the fundamental structure which is shared by the enigma and the mystery, from which follows the eventual status of truth and its indissoluble link to being and nothingness.[18]

We could formalize it as follows. In "Science and Truth", Lacan relates Aristotle's four causes to truths specific to four different fields, namely, magic (efficient cause), science (formal cause), religion (final cause), and psychoanalysis (material cause). Two things may be pointed out. First, and somewhat surprisingly, that art, or creation, is nowhere to be found, which essentially implies that the field of art lacks a proper truth-cause, and, accordingly, that we remain unauthorized to speak of "truths of art"; second, that there is one form of Aristotelian causality that remains unenumerated, given that we choose to perceive it as distinct from the others. It is quite tempting to conjoin them, and to relate them to the revelation. It is the primal cause, which Aristotelian theology conceives of as the cause of the world, and equates with God – as in the cases of Spinoza and the mystics. Here, however, it would be nothing but the revelation *itself* that would be granted the status of truth, owing to its capacity of acting as primal cause of creation, that is, insofar as intuitions are granted a causative status in the creative process characteristic of, but not limited to, art. The revelation would thus be the primal cause that sets the creative process in motion.[19]

We may relate these five forms of truth-causes to five different forms of theistic structures, and, further, to five corresponding techniques, and five characteristic moments in the process of creation; it suffices to say that these divisions are to be regarded as purely heuristic, and it serves only to broadly differentiate between highly schematic characteristics. (1) As Freud states in *Totem and Taboo*, magic is the technique of animism, or polytheism, wherein the efficient truth-causes are related to the incantatory dialogue between man and nature, where, as Lacan asserts, "what must be mobilized in nature [is] thunder and rain, meteors and miracles",[20] that is, the mysterious. Thus, the truth-cause of polytheism is efficient, and appears in the form of the mysterious, which emerges in the (real) encounter, and is manipulated through the technique of magic. (2) In monotheistic religions, the truth-cause is final, or teleological, insofar as it emphasizes moral action and ultimate ends, whose fundamental aims and coordinates are determined by interpretation of Scripture, which is read as a (symbolic) creation, and thus essentially appears in the form of a rebus, which the history of the Abrahamitic religions testifies of. (3) The general structure of pantheism, or panentheism, enables the

Table 5.1 Truth-causes and theistic structures

Structure	Untruth	Event	Cause	Technique	Creation
Polytheism	Mystery	Mysterious	Efficient	Magic	Encountering
Pantheism	Mystery	Revelation	Primal	Meditation	Finding
Monotheism	Enigma	Rebus	Final	Interpretation	Creating
Psychoanalysis	Enigma	Error	Material	Free association	Waiting
Science	Falsity	Anomaly	Formal	Experimentation	Discovering

subject, in a moment of (imaginary) finding, to experience his own divine nature through gnostic revelations, which have the status of primal causes, and which are on occasion induced by mystic meditations (or other mystical practices). (4) In science (which is neither inherently atheistic nor agnostic, but is determined by a particular non-relation to the divine), the truth-cause is being specified as formal, insofar as it remains within the limitations provided by the rigor of theoretical reason (and by falsity), aided by the empirical technique of experimentation, and where creation is bounded by the general structure of discovery (and of the anomalous). (5) Psychoanalysis, lastly, cannot be said to constitute a proper theistic position, but, to complete the schema, we must assert that its truth-cause, owing to the emphasis on the materiality of the signifier, is specified as being material, and which irrupts in the form of the error, which is dealt with through the technique of free association, which requires, as we all know, a great deal of patience, meaning, that the analyst must learn the art of waiting.

Notes

1 Alexandre Kojève, "A Note on Eternity, Time and, the Concept", in *Introductory Lectures on Hegel*, trans. James H. Nichols, Jr. (Ithaca/London: Cornell University Press, 1980), p. 120.
2 Benedict de Spinoza, *Ethics*, trans. Edwin Curley (London: Penguin, 1996), p. 10.
3 This gap we may understand as indicating an epistemological symptom inherent in the Spinozist system, for, on the one hand, Spinoza declares that God "involves no negation" (ID6E; Spinoza, *Ethics*, p. 2), that "there is no vacuum in Nature" (IP15S4, p. 12), and that "being finite is really, in part, a negation, and being infinite is an absolute affirmation" (IP8S1, p. 4); but, on the other hand, it presents no principle whereby the leap is taken from the infinite to the finite, from absolute affirmation to relative negation, other than simply presupposing that the infinite includes all that is finite, and that they are identical on the level of totality (the world). Hence, as in the case of the Neoplatonists, the All (Νοῦς, Divine Intellect; the infinite attribute of thought thinking the infinite idea of God) is at once the unity of the Many (Ψυχή, Soul; interconnected finite modes), which it includes, and the image of the One (τὸ Ἕν; God/substance). In Spinoza's system, there is a gap which cannot possibly exist according to its own fundamental principles, a gap without which no mediating reciprocal causation between or determination of finite modes could take place, since everything finite would be immediately determined affirmatively by the infinite. In psychoanalytic terms, we could say that this reflects the symptomatic status of the oxymoronic real void. What is essentially lacking, and which Spinoza seemingly solves only by arguing that the infinite includes everything finite, is something akin to the Neoplatonist's quasi-cosmogonic *process* of emanation.

In Spinoza, instead of temporal emanation, we find identity through inclusion. However, he does in fact utilize the frequently appearing Neoplatonic metaphor "flow" once in the *Ethics*: "I have shown clearly enough that from God's supreme power, *or* infinite nature, infinitely many things in infinitely many modes, that is, all things, have necessarily flowed" (IP17S1). Spinoza, *Ethics*, p. 14. We may verily ask ourselves if the occurrence of this metaphor is to be regarded as symptomatic.

4

We conceive things as actual in two way: either insofar as we conceive them to exist in relation to a certain time and place, or insofar as we conceive them to be contained in God and to follow from the necessity of the divine nature ... under a species of eternity, and their ideas involve the eternal and infinite essence of God (VP29S).

(Spinoza, *Ethics*, p. 174)

Spinoza formulates this as follows, in terms of the essence and existence of a specific individual: on the one hand, "the essence of man does not involve necessary existence, that is, from the order of Nature [i.e. God] it can happen equally that this or that man does exist, or that he does not exist" (IIA1); but, on the other hand, "nevertheless, in God there is necessarily an idea that expresses the essence of this or that human body, under a species of eternity" (VP22). Spinoza, *Ethics*, pp. 32, 172.

5 Spinoza, *Ethics*, p. 57.
6 Ibid.
7 Ibid. The differentiation between knowledge of the second and the third kind corresponds quite accurately with that between *Binah* ("understanding") and *Chochmah* ("wisdom") of the Kabbalah.
8 Spinoza, *Ethics*, p. 177.
9 As Ibn Arabi said of similar things: "This cannot be comprehended by discursive logic, for this type of knowledge comes only through Divine Intuition". Muhyiddin Ibn Al-'Arabi, *The Seals of Wisdom* (Santa Barbara: Concord Grove Press, 1983), p. 33.
10 Spinoza, *Ethics*, p. 175.
11 Ibid., p. 176.
12 Ibid., p. 180. It is reasonable to assume that Spinoza, on this point, was influenced by Moses Maimonides, who puts forward a similar ethical standpoint revolving around the intellectual love of God in the 51st chapter of *Guide of the Perplexed*.
13 The main difference being that al-Hallaj quite literally said it out loud, affirming that God was him, while Spinoza settled with saying that his eternal essence was eternally in God, which essentially amounts to the same thing.
14 Ludwig Wittgenstein, *Tractatus Logico-Philosophicus*, trans. C. K. Ogden (London: Kegan Paul, 1922), p. 24.
15 Wittgenstein, *Tractatus*, p. 89. My italics. Also: "There is indeed the inexpressible. This *shows* itself; it is the mystical". Wittgenstein, *Tractatus*, p. 90.
16 This could be compared with the revelation that led to Albert Einstein's discovery of general relativity. Einstein retells that he, in 1907, came to realize that a body in free fall would not experience any gravitational field, an insight which led him to postulate the equivalence principle, which states the equivalence between inertial mass and gravitational mass, and that there is no way to distinguish between the force exerted on a body in a gravitational field and the fictitious force which this body would experience in an accelerating frame of reference, which further led him to the thought that spacetime is curved, after which followed several years of arduous work in search for an adequate mathematical formulation that would properly explain his intuition. Famously, he called this insight "the happiest thought of my life", and general relativity as we know it was not "discovered" or presented until 1915–1916. Albert Einstein, "Fundamental Ideas and Methods of the Theory of Relativity, Presented in Their Development", in Albert

Einstein, *The Collected Papers of Albert Einstein. Volume 7. The Berlin Years: Writings 1918–1921*, trans. Alfred Engel (Princeton/Oxford: Princeton University Press, 2002), p. 136.
17 As Ibn Arabi puts it:

In what I have written, I have never had a set purpose, as other writers. Flashes of divine inspiration used to come upon me and almost overwhelm me, so that I could only put them from my mind by committing to paper what they revealed to me. If my works evince any form of composition, it was unintentional. Some works I wrote at the command of God, sent to me in sleep or through mystical revelation.

Cited in R. W. J. Austin, "Introduction", in Ibn Al' Arabi, *The Bezels of Wisdom*, trans. R. W. J. Austin (Mahwah: Paulist Press, 1980), p. 13.
18 This would imply that the truth of the revelation is beyond silence, and therefore it is neither true nor false in terms of language. Critically, it must not be seen as some form of "deeper" truth, or "truer" truth, or inarticulable truth, or, for that sake, as "subjective" in the sense of it being tied to the singular experience of the individual, for it is linked to nothing but *untruth* and thus also to *being*, and is therefore as true as the error, and for exactly the same reason.
19 Fittingly, in the Kabbalah, the second sefirot, *Chochmah*, the divine Wisdom, or intuition, is also called *reshit*, "beginning", owing to it being the primordial force in the creation of the world. Hence, the opening lines of the *Torah*, "*Be-reshit bara Elohim*...", "In the beginning God created...", are also interpreted as "with wisdom God created...". See, for example, the account of the creation of the world in the *Zohar*:

At the head of potency of the King [*Ein Sof*], He engraved engravings in luster on high [*Keter*]. A spark of impenetrable darkness flashed within the concealed of the concealed, from the head of Infinity – a cluster of vapor forming in formlessness, thrust in a ring, not white, not black, not red, not green, no color at all. As a cord surveyed, it yielded radiant colors. Deep within the spark gushed a flow, splaying colors below, concealed within the concealed of the mystery of *Ein Sof*. It split and did not split its aura, was not known at all, until under the impact of splitting, a single, concealed, supernal point shone [*Chochmah*]. Beyond that point, nothing is known, so it is called *Reshit, Beginning*, first command of all.

Daniel C. Matt (ed.), *Zohar. Pritzker Edition. Volume One*, trans. Daniel C. Matt (Stanford: Stanford University Press, 2004), p. 107ff.
20 Jacques Lacan, "Science and Truth", in *Écrits*, trans. Bruce Fink (New York/London: W. W. Norton & Company, 2006), p. 740.

Chapter 6
Blahblahcan *avico* Vico

> My proofs are of a divine kind and should therefore,
> O reader, give you a divine pleasure.[1]
>
> Giambattista Vico, *Scienza Nuova*

Psychoanalysis has imposed a sort of linguistic taboo upon itself: it is forbidden to speak of the birth of language. Everything that may be said about this origin presupposes its own dimension; every logo-genetic hypothesis is but a myth inscribed in the domain whose very existence it attempts to explain. Its "before" is inscribed "within"; historical time is cut off from its presumably transcendent "real" time. It is a story about itself in itself. But "it" is not equal to "its" "self". There is no metalanguage, hence every auto-genetic narrative implies an implicit metaphysical hypostatization, situating the world of the word in the world. But there is a gap between these worlds, and this gap is not of Spinozist nature: although the symbolic and the real are in some sense "parallel", substantial equivalence is out of question. The symbolic is the dimension of the hole, but there is no hole before the emergence of the symbolic. The symbolic creates the very hole which it presupposes. The symbolic drills the hole that enables it to oscillate, circulate, operate – "the fashioning of the signifier and the introduction of a gap or a hole in the real are identical".[2] Accordingly, the prohibition of logo-genesis is supplemented by a sort of negative meta-myth. As there cannot be any hole in the real that precedes the signifier, it is necessary to speak about the conditions of the creation of the hole which cannot exist without the signifier which cannot exist without the hole. Instead of the unity of the symbolic and the real that metaphysical logo-genesis presumably implies, we are forced to acknowledge the original "unity" of the symbolic and the hole, that is, their primordial simultaneous emergence. Thus, we must choose between evolutionary naivety and monotheistic cowardice, between metaphysical logo-genesis and quasi-theological *ex nihilo*. Psychoanalysis has chosen the latter. The signifier and the hole instantly come into being through the creation of the "first" signifier which signifies nothing but "nothing". The vase.

> The potter ... creates the vase with his hand around this emptiness, creates it, just like the mythical creator, *ex nihilo*, starting with a hole. ... If it really is a

signifier, and the first of such signifiers fashioned by human hand, it is in its signifying essence a signifier of nothing other than of signifying as such, or, in other words, of no particular signifier. ... This nothing in particular that characterizes it in its signifying function is that which in its incarnated form characterizes the vase as such. It creates the void and thereby introduces the possibility of filling it. It is on the basis of this fabricated signifier, this vase, that emptiness and fullness as such enter the world.[3]

The vase im-ports the hole. Problem solved.

This perspective proceeds from the presumption that there cannot be any hole in the real "before" the symbolic. I wish to challenge this conception by putting forward a third alternative: neither naivety nor cowardice – stupidity.

Let me tell you a little story. Once upon a time...

The Sublime Poetry of the Mute Baby Giants

In the beginning, before the Word, there was a primal horde of hairy gorillas. Or, better perhaps, there were dispersed hideous giants, as the Italian philosopher Giambattista Vico (1668–1744) would have it. These giants were "stupid, insensate, and horrid beast",[4] and their huge stature derived from their barbaric mothers not cleaning them, abandoning them to absorb their own "nitrous salts"[5] and grow large just like plants and trees. The giants were mute, yet they did not suffer from their aphasia: they wandered around the world's great forest without ever encountering each other; speech was not of any use to them. They could not speak, hence they could not think. They did not understand anything. They could, however, scream, stutter, and sing, which they often did when affected by sense impressions or emotions; the less the giants understood, the stronger the emotions and the more they stuttered and sang. The giants were also by nature great mimics and endowed with a vivid imagination; the stronger the emotions, the more they imagined. Further, when the emotions elicited by impressions from the external world became overwhelming, the giants felt wonder and imagined that the cause of these emotions was a living entity, even a god. And since they did not understand anything about these gods, they believed that they were just like themselves. Thus, the giants understood nothing and became overwhelmed by everything and imitated everything and fantasized about everything and believed that everything was gods that were just like themselves while screaming, stuttering, singing, and strolling around all alone in the world.[6]

Babies cannot speak or think; they understand nothing. They can, however, scream, stutter, sing, imagine, and imitate, just like giants. Further, the joy which babies derive from playing lies in them imagining things as if they were living entities, just like the giants when they imagined things as being gods; in fact, the main difference between giants and babies seems to be their size. Moreover, the most sublime thing about poetry is that it imagines inanimate things as if they had feelings, which the mute giants did all the time. Thus spoke Giambattista:

> The most sublime task of poetry is to give sense and passion to insensate objects. It is a characteristic of children to pick up inanimate objects and speak to them while playing as if they were living persons. This philological-philosophical axiom proves that men living in the world's childhood were by nature sublime poets.[7]

And thus he spoke of the origin of the sublime poetry of the mute baby giants:

> The word "logic" comes from λόγος, "logos", which originally signified *"favola"*, "fable", which later changed into Italian *"favela"*, "speech" – fable in Greek was μῦθος, "myth", which is the root of Latin *"mutus"*, "mute" – for speech arose in the mute epoch as a mental language which ... existed before spoken or articulated languages: this is why λόγος means both "idea" and "word" ... The first speech of the nations in the mute times must have begun as signs or gestures or things which stood in a natural relation to the ideas they expressed. Hence λόγος or Latin *"verbum"* also signified "thing", and in Hebrew also meant "deed" ... The first speech, which was spoken by the theological poets, was not a speech in accordance with the nature of things ... but rather a *fantastical speech based on animate substances*, most of which they imagined to be divine.[8]

The mute baby giants roamed the world in the times following the great flood, when all of the world's water submerged the Earth; but when the water started to evaporate, huge clouds formed in the sky. Then, for the first time during their lives, the giants encountered the strangest and most overwhelming phenomenon they had ever witnessed – lightning. The mute baby giants were afraid of these remarkable bolts, and they did not understand anything about them, and since they believed that everything that they did not understand was like themselves, they thought that the sound of thunder sounded like their stuttering, screams, and songs, and therefore they believed that the sky was a god who made sounds with clouds and that the sounds were bolts and that the god "was trying to speak to them through the whistling of his bolts and the crashing of his thunder"[9] and that this god was called Jupiter. Then, they began to imitate the speech of the god Jupiter. Thus spoke Giambattista:

> Articulate language began to take shape in onomatopoeia, which we still find children happily using to express themselves. In Latin, Jupiter was initially called *Ious*, from the roar of the thunder; in Greek, "Ζεύς", after the whistle of the lightning; in the East, *"Ur"*, after the sound of burning fire, from which derives *Urim*, the power of fire; this must be the origin of Greek ουρανός, heaven, and Latin "uro", "to burn". The whistle of the lightning must also have given rise to Latin *cel*, heaven ... Hence it is not unlikely that, after the thunderbolts awaked

the wonder of mankind, Jupiter's exclamations gave rise to the first exclamation produced by the human voice: "*pa!*".[10]

Then words imitated themselves, just like when you stutter, and so heaven became papa. The mute baby giants thought that everything in nature sounded strange, and therefore they thought that everything was a god, and that "nature was Jupiter's language",[11] and that that the words of the nature speech of the god papa Jupiter were things, which they, overwhelmed by wonder, imagined to be just like themselves:

> That which is metaphysics insofar as it contemplates things in all the forms of their being, is logic insofar as it considers things in all the forms by which they may be signified. Accordingly, as poetry has been considered by us above as a poetic metaphysics, in which the theological poets imagined bodies to be for the most part divine substances, so now that same poetry is considered as poetic logic, by which it signifies them. ... The most luminous and therefore the most necessary and frequent [figure] is metaphor. It is most praised when it gives sense and passion to insensate things, in accordance with the metaphysics above discussed, by which the first poets attributed to bodies the being of animate substances, with capacities measured by their own, namely sense and passion, and in this way made fables of them. Thus every metaphor so formed is a fable in brief. ... [So man] made of himself an entire world. So that, as rational metaphysics teaches that man becomes all things by understanding them (*homo intelligendo fit omnia*), this imaginative metaphysics shows that man becomes all things by not understanding them (*homo non intelligendo fit omnia*); and perhaps the latter proposition is truer than the former, for when man understands he extends his mind and takes in the things, but when he does not understand he makes the things out of himself and becomes them by transforming himself into them.[12]

Thus, proceeding from their poetic metaphysics, which transformed the world to a musical mirror populated by gods, the mute baby giants started to speak by singing and stuttering in metaphors. This was the first speech of humanity, their own poetic logic, their sublime response to the nature speech of the God papa Jupiter, which arose naturally from their inborn stupidity. But as time went, and the mute baby giants became less stupid, they went on to name all the things in nature proceeding from these metaphors:

> Using their poetic logic, which was a product of poetic metaphysics, the early poetic people named things in two ways: (1) by using sensible ideas, which are the source of metonymy; and (2) by using particular ideas, which are the source of synecdoche. ... For example, the theological poets understood Jupiter, Cybele or Berecynthia, and Neptune in this way. At first, pointing mutely, they interpreted them as the substances of the sky, earth, and sea, which they imagined to be animate deities ... Later, as their vast imagination diminished and their

powers of abstraction increased, these deities shrank to diminutive symbols of themselves. Since the origin of these human institutions were buried in obscurity, metonymy dressed these symbols in the learned guise of allegory. Jupiter grew so small and light that an eagle now carries him in its flight. Neptune rides the sea in a dainty coach. And Cybele is seated on a lion.[13]

By this time, the mute baby giants were completely impious; there were no social bonds, no families, no nations, and no moral, and thus they felt no shame for their passions, which they acted on uninhibited when meeting by chance while strolling around all alone in the world. In fact, "in their nefarious feral wanderings ... bestial venery was practiced by sons with mothers and by fathers with daughters".[14] However, the nature speech of the god papa Jupiter sounded frightening, and therefore the giants felt the urge to understand them by divining their signification, as well as those of other divine sounds of nature, the language of the gods, by singing in metaphors and metonymies. So, proceeding from their poetic metaphysics, they divined that the bolts were expressions of the wrath of the God papa Jupiter, and thus "it was in the heavens that men first read the laws dictated by lightning bolts".[15] Nevertheless, the giants remained afraid of these bolts to the degree that they withdrew from the open lands and forests into caves by the mountains, where they settled down, and, for the first time in history, entered into social relations. Thus spoke Giambattista:

> By their fearful religion of thunderbolts, the giants checked their bestial habit of wandering wild through the earth's great forest. ... They now settled down, hidden away in their lands (*fondi*), so that they later became the founders (*fondatori*) of the nations ... The virtue of the spirit began to grow, and kept them from satisfying their bestial lust in the sight of Heaven, which now inspired their mortal fear. Instead, each giant would drag a woman into his cave and keep her there as his lifelong mate. In this way, they practiced human intercourse secretly in private, which is to say, with modesty and shame. ... In this manner, marriage was introduced, which we may define as a *carnal union modestly consummated in fear of some divinity.*[16]

This was the birth of civilization. The giants learned how to love. In the vicinity of these caves, the baby giants, which by now began acting piously, came to found the first cities, after having gathered in search of protection from the wrath of the god papa Jupiter. But since they had ceased to wander away from each other, they were confronted with the fact of death. Where the giants lived, they also died:

> The pious giants who settled in the mountains must have noticed the stench which arose from the corpses of their dead as they rotted on the ground nearby, and must have begun to bury their dead. The pious giants imbued their tombs with such great religious awe, or fear of the divine, that the Latin expression *locus religius*, hallowed ground, came primarily to mean a cemetery. This was

the origin of the universal belief in the immortality of human souls ... [Hence], the Latin word for civilization, *humanitas*, derives from the verb *humare*, to bury. ... [And] through protracted settlement and the burial of their ancestors, they came to found and divide the first dominions of the earth. The lords of these domains were called giants, a Greek word which means "sons of the earth", or descendants of the buried dead.[17]

But owing to them now living together in their settlements, the pious giants also felt the stench of the living, and since they thought that the god papa Jupiter thought just like them, they interpreted the thundering heavens as commanding cleanliness. This led the giants to clean themselves, and the mothers, who no longer abandoned their children to wallow in their nitrous salts, to clean them too:

> It was in the cleansing of their bodies, together with the fear of the gods and their fathers – fears quite terrifying in a primitive age – which caused the giants to shrink to our natural stature. This is perhaps why the Latin adjective *politus*, cleansed or neat, derives from Greek *politeia*, civil government.[18]

Thus we ceased to be mute baby giants, according to Giambattista Vico.

Was Vico Mad?

Needless to say, the theory of the origin of language of Giambattista Vico, this sublimely bizarre deviation in the history of Western thought, is, three centuries after its conception, far beyond untenable – but, simultaneously, we cannot, in the midst of this wonderful mess, fail to acknowledge his remarkable originality and far-reaching clear-sightedness. At times, Vico was centuries before his time: it is well-established that he was the first philosopher of history; that he was the first to propose a "constructivist" epistemology (*Verum esse ipsum factum*, "truth is precisely what is made"[19]), two centuries before the French tradition; that he was the first to argue for the cyclical nature of history, half a century before Hegel; that he was the first to assert that class struggle was one of the main driving forces of history, a century before Marx; that he was the first to propose such like narratives about the poetic, musical, or imitative origin of language, several decades before Rousseau and Herder[20]; that he was the only to argue for the simultaneity of the origin of speech and writing, two centuries before Derrida[21]; that he arguably inaugurated the genre of philosophical autobiography in writing *The Life of Giambattista Vico Written by Himself*; that he was one of the first, if not the first, to integrate etymology with philosophy; and that his use of language influenced the style and structure of the writing of James Joyce.[22] Clearly, his peers had their reasons to essentially ignore all of his ideas, but perhaps the history of Western thought, nevertheless, justifies what he himself seems to suggest in the first page of his autobiography, avowedly written as neutral as possible, and in third person – that he was a genius. Were we to apply this useless category on him, then we must verily ask ourselves if he was not a mad one. Moreover, if we maintain that Lacan did right in raising the question "Was Joyce mad?",[23] this must certainly apply for Vico as well. Accordingly, we could arguably perceive his philosophy as his "proper" sinthome, and, given that Joyce's sinthome sheds light on the language of the unconscious, it would not be unreasonable to suggest the very same thing for Vico's – not least owing to their similarities, and to the influence of Vico on Joyce. Whatever may be the case, it is of secondary importance for our purposes. What Vico's philosophy says about Vico does not matter. The only question I wish to raise is what Vico may say about psychoanalysis. And if we are to follow Lacan in arguing that Freud's discovery of the unconscious anticipated the theory of structural linguistics, particularly by emphasizing the operations displacement (metonymy) and condensation (metaphor), we may doubtless add to the long list of Vico's anticipations comparative anthropology, structural linguistics, and, which is what is at stake for us, and perhaps even to a greater degree than anyone else in the history of philosophy and science, the psychoanalysis of Freud and Lacan.[24] Would it be inadequate to argue that we may interpret Vico's poetic metaphysics and poetic logic as essentially describing the dynamics of the unconscious? This is precisely what I will attempt to argue for – and, further, that he may shed new light on some significant lacunas in psychoanalytic theory, opening up a path which enables us to go beyond its self-imposed limitations concerning the origin and nature of language.

Freud's Poetic Metaphysics

Freud spoke of the psychoanalytic work as an excavation, and Vico of his discovery of the wisdom of the ancients as an unearthing. In both cases, what they discovered, and had to reconstruct, was the deeply buried, forgotten origins of human thought. For Freud, it was the thought processes of the unconscious, illuminated by the psychology of children, and its symptomatic presence in the mental life of the adult in the form of "repetitions and reactions dating from infancy";[25] for Vico, it was the language of the giants, "the children of the human race",[26] mirroring that of the infant, and its presence in the rational "age of men", as he puts it, in the form of poetry. Hence, for both Freud and Vico, what is at stake is a form of truth that is essentially *historical*, precisely owing to it being forgotten – but simultaneously, that which is forgotten is "simpler", so to speak, than the long, arduous process of forgetting, for this process is one of ongoing *mediation*, of psychic-historic ontogenetic-phylogenetic work and dissimulation, resulting in the loss of the immediate simplicity of that which lies at the origin.[27] In other words, although that which is to be reconstructed, from the point of view of "rational" thought, may appear to be highly implausible, untenable, or speculative, and can be reconstructed only through laborious work of interpretation, this truth can to a much greater degree may be taken, in all its naivety, "for what it is", due to it simply reflecting the unmediated, undistorted, concrete nature of the psychology of children. In the words of Vico:

> Since the pagan world's earliest people were as simple as children, who are by nature truthful, they could invent nothing false in their early myths. These myths must therefore have been *true narratives* ... The meaning of their allegories is based on identity rather than analogy, and is thus historical rather than philosophical.[28]

Onto the topic of psychosexual "development". I will not fall to the temptation of allegorically interpreting the beginning of Vico's "theoretical myth" vulgarly, viewing the origin of gigantism, which would reflect the "grandiosity" of the ego of primary narcissism, as stemming from auto-eroticism, owing to the children's absorption of their own "nitrous salts". However, although their originary myths in terms of drives and passions clearly diverge in several significant aspects, it is also crucial to point out some similarities: Freud's myth revolve around the repression of polymorphous enjoyment and incestuous desires through the constitution of totemism, the first religious institution of civilization, a symbolic substitute for the tyrannical primal Father; while for Vico, it concerns the taming of disordered passions, which contain incestuous elements – "incest is the execrable abomination of the lawless world"[29] – through the constitution of religion and the family, the first two institutions of humankind, under the frightful rule of Jupiter, the universal primordial Father of humankind – and, furthermore, and as a consequence of this, the leap from self-love to love of the other. As he puts it:

> In his bestial state, a man loves only his own well-being. After he takes a wife and has children, he continues to love his own well-being, and comes to love the well-being of his family a well.[30]

This evidently corresponds to the evolution from the narcissistic stage of the libido to that of object-love, which correlates with the development of civilization from animism to religion:

> The animistic phase would correspond to narcissism both chronologically and in its content; the religious [Oedipal] phase would correspond to the stage of object-choice of which the characteristic is a child's attachment to his parents.[31]

Which leads us to the central point. There are surprisingly exact overlaps between Vico's poetic metaphysics and Freud's perspective on animism. Concerning this, Vico clearly anticipates the anthropology of Tylor and Frazer by one and a half century. The essence of Vico's poetic metaphysics is that human beings, when lacking access to rational language, remain ignorant of everything, and thus transpose their whole psychology into nature, thereby making themselves the measure of the universe, encountering themselves, without being conscious of it, everywhere in the world, in the guise of gods and spirits: "they made a deity ... of everything that exceeded their limited understanding".[32] The first world-view of the history of humanity, that of "the age of gods", is based on nothing but this imaginative poetic metaphysics. Freud, on his part, likewise understood animism, the all-encompassing world-view wherein humans endowed life and spirit to everything in nature, as a result of human beings "transposing the structural conditions of his own mind into the external world",[33] which he specified as being caused by "the projection outwards of internal perceptions",[34] at least partially owing to them not having access to any "language of abstract thought ... [which would enable] sensory residues of verbal presentations [to be] linked to the internal processes".[35] Being based on projection, this world-view is essentially *paranoid* in nature:

> Spirits and demons ... are only projections of man's own emotional impulses. He turns his emotional cathexes into persons, he peoples the world with them and meets his internal mental processes again outside himself – in just the same way as that intelligent paranoiac, Schreber, found a reflection of the attachments and detachments of his libido in the vicissitudes of his confabulated "rays of God".[36]

In other words, Schreber's divine sun rays are, just like the experience of the encounter with spirits and demons in animism, "nothing else than a concrete representation and projection outwards of libidinal cathexes",[37] which, further, as Freud briefly asserts in a footnote to in his case study on him, are "identical with the voices which talked the 'basic language' ",[38] the language of God. We may in passing mention the striking affinity between these sun rays and Vico's rays of lighting, which spoke the concrete primordial language of Jupiter, to the degree that it would even be possible to argue that we, in Vico, take part in a properly proto-psychoanalytic description of the general structure of paranoia.

Crucially, the world-view corresponding to Vico's poetic metaphysics and Freud's account of animism agree on this central aspect: the world is a mirror for the soul. For both, it is conditioned by the lack of abstract or rational language – and thus it *cannot* properly be understood in terms of it. Although this lack verily "liberates" the poetic metaphysics of animism, it is but a *retroactive* precondition – prosaic language comes *afterwards*, tames it, but it must nevertheless be understood as such, in "itself", in its proper right. Perhaps the sovereignty of the mirror is bound to be overthrown by reason, but of this, the mirror knows nothing – not yet, and thus "yet" does not exist. In other words: although it is conditioned by the absence of repression, animism is based on projection, and not non-repression[39]; and, although it is conditioned by ignorance, poetic metaphysics it is based the imaginative faculties, not non-rationality.

On this point, we may identify a lacuna in Freud. The phenomena pertaining to animism are all dependent on the absence of a prosaic language for the internal psychological processes – but what is the nature of the speech that precedes it? Freud says nothing about the language corresponding to animism. He speaks of its "metaphysics", or *Weltanschauung*, but he does not specify what kind of speech predated the "language of abstract thought" of the religious and scientific world-views, what there could be in the place which the "verbal presentations linked to the internal processes" is destined to occupy. Otherwise stated, Freud says nothing about the nature of the language of non-abstract – that is, *concrete* – verbal presentations linked to the *external* processes whose signification is primarily, and *a priori*, determined by the transposition of the mind into the inanimate through projection, except perhaps as implicitly, vaguely, and briefly indicated as a distant association in the short footnote on Schreber reiterated above. For Vico, this is the essence of poetry. It is what antedates the prose of the age of men, the language of religion, philosophy, and science. Animism is the metaphysics of poetry. It lies at its core. There can be no poetry without it. It speaks of that which is within as if it were without, owing to the simple fact that within and without, under the guise of allegory, are identical. In Freud, everything is there – but there is something missing on the level of language. The metaphysics of animism does not correspond to any form of definite "logic". More specifically, for Freud, there is no link whatsoever between the animistic phenomena pertaining to this lack of abstract language and a form of logic which we could conceive of as being associated with poetry – and thus there is no logic that could render the metaphysics of animism "poetic". Perhaps this lacuna indicates the site of a question that needs to be raised.

Lacan's Poetic Logic

Onto Lacan. To begin, it is necessary to dwell upon two salient affinities between Vico and Lacan: first, the correlation between Vico's poetic logic and the functioning and effectivity peculiar to Lacan's formulation of the unconscious; second, the similarity between what for both of them is given the status of a form of pre-discursive verbality, which for Lacan goes under the name *lalangue*.

Now, it may be mentioned that Vico is generally considered as the first to propose that all rhetoric figures are ultimately reducible to what two centuries after the writing of *Scienza Nuova* came to be referred to as the four "master tropes". He asserts:

> All figures of speech may be reduced to these four types – metaphor, metonymy, synecdoche, and irony – which were previously thought to be the ingenious inventions of writers. By my discussions of them proves that they were in fact necessary modes of expression in all the early poetic nations, and originally had natural and proper meanings. These expressions became figurative only later, as the human mind developed and invented words which signified abstract forms … Knowing this, we may begin to demolish two common errors of the grammarians: that prose is the proper form of speech, and poetic speech improper; and that men spoke first in prose and later in verse.[40]

Language is intrinsically, and primordially, poetic, and the tropes, which serve as its operational fundament, are by no means mere supplements or ornaments, but essential to its proper functioning. Moreover, since the original speech of early humankind was based on identity and must hence be considered as naively "true", Vico points out that "irony could clearly arise only in an age capable of reflection, because it consists of a falsehood which reflection disguises in a mask of truth";[41] and, furthermore, if we follow the general standpoint of contemporary linguistics and perceive synecdoche as a variation of metonymy, we could assert that Vico was the first to propose that the functioning of language is originally and ultimately based on the poetic tropes metaphor and metonymy, as would Jakobson and Lacan maintain two centuries later.[42]

Moreover, for Vico, the domain of language and institutions – the symbolic order – is the proper locus of history. Hence, transformations in and of language do not only reflect or correlate with real historical or cultural transformations, but are, in some sense, these transformations themselves. Accordingly, etymologic chains based on polyvalence, homonymity, equivocality, literality, and similitude mirror, or even constitute, the causal chains in question:

> [The] sequence of human things sets the pattern for the histories of words ... Thus we observe in the Latin language that almost the whole corpus of its words had sylvan or rustic origins. For example, *lex*. First it must have meant "collection of acorns." Thence we believe is derived *ilex*, as it were *illex*, "the oak" (as certainly *aquilex* is the "collector of waters"); for the oak produces the acorns by which the swine [*hys* in Greek] are drawn together [hence *hylex*]. *Lex* was next "a collection of vegetables", from which the latter were called *legumina*. Later on, at a time when vulgar letters had not yet been invented for writing down the laws, *lex* by a necessity of civil nature must have meant "a collection of citizens" ... Finally collecting letters, and making as it were a sheaf of them in each word, was called *legere*, "reading".[43]

It is of lesser importance that Vico's examples suffer from a certain tendency to be comically implausible. Who would maintain that *humanitas*, humanity or civilization, derives from *humare*, to bury, owing to the belief in the soul and its immortality derives from funeral rites; that *mutus*, mute, derives from *mythos*, myth, owing to the first speech, being properly mythical, emerged in the mute epoch; or that cleansed, *politus*, derives from *politeia*, government, owing to the constitution of the latter imposed rudimentary rules concerning hygiene? What matters here is not the believability of Vico's exemplifications, but the fact that the form of effectivity which they make manifest is based on the very same form of causal phonetic-metonymic contiguity that is essential to the functioning of the Freudian unconscious as interpreted and articulated by Lacan – that of the wit. Vico's poetic logic is structured like a language in Lacan's sense of the term; the causality of the historical development of civilization according to Vico overlaps with that of the production of the symptom according to Lacan. And just as in the case of Lacan, Vico situates this form of metonymic effectivity at the heart of his interpretative methodology: "I have directed my attention to unearthing the most ancient wisdom of the Italians ... from the very origins of their words".[44] Otherwise stated, for Vico, just as for Lacan, that which is forgotten in the domain of language is "excavated" through the interpretation of metaphors, metonymies, and polyvalences deriving from the phonetic materiality of words.

Which leads us to *lalangue*. Of this, Lacan says:

> What I put forward, by writing *lalangue*, as one word, is that by which I distinguish myself from structuralism, insofar as the latter would like to integrate language into semiology. ... If I have said that language is what the unconscious is structured like, that is because language, first of all, doesn't exist. Language is what we try to know concerning the function of *lalangue*.[45]

Lacan draws the line of demarcation which separates him from the structuralist conception of language, according to which the signifier is conceived of as difference, as pure negativity – for language gathers all of its negative elements from *lalangue*, understood as a form of substantialized, "positive" non-discursive verbality; the differential structure of language lifts all of its constituents from the undifferentiated phonetic sea of *lalangue*, which enunciates *not* signifying articulations following the poetic logic of the discourse of the Other, but non-communicative phonations in the service of *jouissance*. In *lalangue*, "speech" is not verbalized, but vocalized, and although language has everything to do with *lalangue*, owing to it being "a knowing how to do things with *lalangue*",[46] *lalangue* has nothing to do with language. It does not refer, it does not signify. It *sounds*. It operates on a wholly different level than that of the signifier; it pertains to the field of *jouissance*, and, as Lacan puts it, produces "effects that are affects", "affects that remain enigmatic"[47] from the point of view of the signifier, due to the simple fact that they are radically beyond its reach. How, then, does *lalangue* sound? Listen to the infant: he screams, he stutters, he sings, he babbles, he repeats, he imitates. Why? Because he enjoys, suffers, feels. Because of pain and joy. Because it feels good. There is nothing more and nothing less to it. It has no meaning. In *lalangue*, *jouissance* gives life to the voice by sounding, like songs without words, and from these wordless songs, words borrow their substance. Hence the "la la la" of the singer, the "blah blah blah" of the speaker, the "la di da" of the snob, the "ha ha ha" of the laugher, the musicality of poetry, the stuttering of truth, and the irreducible import of phonetic equivocality and polysemy.

Lalangue is the name which Lacan gives to that which Vico speaks of as the language of the mute epoch. Like infants, the mute giants had no words – yet they did not remain silent. Owing to their overwhelming passions, they screamed, they stuttered, they sang, they babbled, they repeated, they imitated. Why? Because they enjoyed, suffered, felt. Because of pain and joy. Because it felt good. There was nothing more and nothing less to it. It had no meaning:

> Since men are shown to have been originally mute, they must have uttered vowel sounds by singing, as mutes do; and later, like stammerers, they must have uttered articulate consonantal sounds, still by singing. ... The first dull-witted men were moved to utterance only be very violent passions, which are naturally expressed in a very loud voice. And nature brings it about that when man greatly raises his voice, he breaks into diphthongs and song. ... [Thus] this first song of the people sprang naturally from the difficulty of their first utterances ... under the impulse of most violent passions, even as we still observe men sing when moved by great passions, especially extreme happiness or grief. ... [And thus,] by a necessity of human nature, poetic style arose before prose style; just as, by the same necessity, the fables, or imaginative universals, arose before the rational philosophic universals which were formed through the medium of prose speech.[48]

Hence the "la la la" of the singer... And the irreducible import of phonetic equivocality and polysemy.

I believe that enough has been said about the convergence of Lacan and Vico as to their views of speech and language: on the one hand, they speak of a form of poetic logic that is ultimately based on metaphor and metonymy, and not on prose or reason; on the other, they speak of a form of pre-discursive verbality that is based on *jouissance*, musicality, and phonetic equivocality, and not on meaning or communication. Nevertheless, Vico may enable us to identify a significant lacuna in Lacan. Lacan's conception of language and *lalangue* concern only the symbolic and the real. What is crucial to point out is the fact that the irruption of *lalangue* in the "development" of the infant occurs roughly at the time as the "phase" where his experience of the world is dominated by the imaginary – the mirror stage. Somehow, there seems to be a non-relation between the functioning of the mirror and *lalangue*, implying, in essence, that they are to be regarded as parallel – this is an implicit corollary to the silence of Lacan. We may verily ask ourselves – why? Is the imaginary, regarding this topic in particular, plainly insignificant, or is it being forgotten, displaced, repressed, even foreclosed? Or, is it unthinkable to go so far as to suggest that it indicates an inherent, and symptomatic, insufficiency in the theory of Lacan, concerning the evanescence of the imaginary owing to the emphasis on the signifier and *jouissance*? Whatever may be the case, Vico may have something to say about what is missing.

For Vico, it is unthinkable to conceive of the essence of logic as poetic without first dwelling upon its peculiar metaphysics, which is wholly based on the imaginary. In animism, the signifier signifies that which the mirror has already projected into the inanimate; logic is poetic owing to it already being predicated by the divinization of the external world through projection. This is why metaphor, to a greater degree than any definition or proposition, is ultimately, under the guise of difference, based on identity – metaphor is immediate. For Lacan, the very opposite is the case. Metaphor and metonymy act upon signifiers only. Metaphor substitutes one signifier for another, producing secondary effects on the imaginary. For Lacan, metaphor is ultimately, under the guise of identity, based on difference. Thus, metaphor essentially excludes the imaginary from the proper realm of poetry: Lacan's poetic logic is a logic without metaphysics, given that the latter is specified as being determined by the sovereignty of the mirror in animism or the mirror stage. Hence the rift that separates Vico's and Lacan's views on poetry. And were we to propose that there is only one form of poetry, and that this poetry is unthinkable without poetic metaphysics, we would be obliged to assert that Jacobson and Lacan, by reducing the functioning of language to the purely linguistic poetic tropes metaphor and metonymy, effectively de-poetize it. I see no reason to suggest such a thing. There is the poetics of the wit, and the poetics of the gods. Both presuppose *lalangue*. But only one of them presupposes poetic metaphysics.

The Nature of Language

So, we have three different phenomena to take into consideration: the paranoid poetic metaphysics of animism and the mirror stage, the poetic logic founded on the operations metaphor and metonymy, and *lalangue*. In Freud, we have poetic metaphysics, but no poetic logic or *lalangue* which would render it poetic; in Lacan, the contrary is the case, since his conceptions of poetic logic and *lalangue* exclude poetic metaphysics. Vico enables us to identify a space left empty in, and by, psychoanalysis: the lieu where Freud and Lacan may supplement each other's lacunas, where poetic metaphysics and poetic logic coalesce.

The problem may be formulated as follows: how to articulate psychoanalytically the relation between poetic metaphysics and poetic logic proceeding from *lalangue*? Vico's answer indicates the path which would lead us forward: *lalangue* is the language of the gods. As Johann Gottfried Herder, who surely must have read Vico, formulates it:

> Speak the word, and like a throng of ghosts those connotations arise of a sudden in their dark majesty from the grave of the soul. ... But take the word away, and the sound of sentiment sounds on. Dark emotion overwhelm us; the frivolous tremble and shudder – not in reaction to thoughts but to syllables, the sounds of childhood; and it was the magic power of the orator, of the poet, that returned us to being children. ... [And] since all of nature sounds, nothing is more natural to a sensuous human being than to think that it lives, that it speaks, that it acts. ... Everywhere gods, goddesses, acting beings of evil or of good. The howling storm and the sweet zephyr, the clear source and the mighty ocean – [the] entire mythology [of man] lies in the treasure trove, the verbs and nouns of the old languages, and the oldest dictionary was thus a sounding pantheon.[49]

Hence, the original treasure trove of signifiers is not the Other, but the realm of the Others of the Other, of the ones – *nature*. For just like children, the world speaks *lalangue*. And for the very same reason: passion. Owing to the mirror.

In *lalangue*, the child does not dialogue with the Other. He dialogues with the world, wordlessly. The child and the world speak the same language, that of the gods, for just like the child, the world screams, stutters, sings, babbles, repeats, imitates. Owing to the mirror.

Lalangue does not signify. There is no need for it. For in poetic metaphysics, the sounding gods are already the child. Owing to the mirror.

Or, rather, owing to the mirror, the sounding gods become the child due to him not being them – this is what must be accounted for psychoanalytically.

Vico distinguishes between mute and articulate language. Articulate language is the prosaic asymptote of poetic logic, accomplished by the de-poetization of language by language through the abandonment of poetic metaphysics, resulting in the forgetting of its poetic fundament.[50] Mute language is the wordless *lalangue* of the gods, insofar as poetic metaphysics makes out of the speaker the sounding pantheon through projection. Poetic metaphysics is conditioned by ignorance, understood in terms of lack of rational language – but muteness and ignorance are not identical. That which sounds in nature sounds from afar. Between the speaker and that which sounds, there is emptiness. Therein, sounds ring. In relation to emptiness, ignorance is a void in the field of language, a hole in the symbolic – silence. In silence, the speaker has no words for that which he does not understand, that which appears and sounds in emptiness. It concerns the unnameable. Muteness, however, indicates something that has nothing to do neither with rational language nor with silence – it regards not words but sounds, pointing toward the void beyond silence, the void wherein they reverberate. In this void, the speaker has no images for that which he does not understand. It concerns the unimaginable.

"In the beginning was the thunder", Samuel Beckett wrote about Vico, "the thunder set free Religion, in its most objective and unphilosophical form – idolatrous animism".[51] From afar, lightning strikes – *pa!* This is what I have spoken of in terms of the encounter with the unimaginable, with the mysterious, with the indifferent, with a one, with a god, with the Other of the Other. In the face of the unimaginable, man is overwhelmed by wonder, by shock and awe, for the unimaginable, appearing in the disjunction of the real and the imaginary, mirrors nothing. It does not signify – it intimates. Into the void beyond silence, he projects himself, creating a god in the image of himself, endowed with life and spirit, just like himself. It sounds and feels, just like himself, and it sounds because it feels, just like himself. Nevertheless, it remains beyond silence, and beyond the reach of the mirror. He projects himself into the unimaginable, but the unimaginable does not mirror him back. It remains a god, for although it is him, he is not it. Then, it disappears. The heavens open. Silence. But the sound of sentiment rings on. And man knows that what he saw was true.

But the unimaginable reappears. Everything in the world stutters. The world repeats. The repetition automatism of the world. The unimaginable oscillates in emptiness, between presence and absence – just like a signifier. As does the revolving sky, the sun, the stars, the moon – soundlessly. Hence, the sun, the stars, the moon speak *lalangue*, for all that the world speaks does not sound. The heavens stutter soundlessly – the music of the spheres. "Astrology [was] the science of the speech of the stars",[52] Vico states, Why? Because they appear and disappear, periodically, just like signifiers – but without signifying, but intimating, for they repeat not in language, but beyond silence.[53]

This is how we should understand *l'inconscient à ciel ouvert de la psychose*, "the unconscious open to the sky": in psychosis, the heavens, in speaking *lalangue*, assume the role of the nature of the unconscious.[54]

The sun, the stars, the moon speak *lalangue*, just like the mother. *Lalangue* is the mother tongue owing to the mother appearing and disappearing in the place of the open sky, in the emptiness of the world. But the mother is not a god, for the gods mirror nothing, whereas the mother mirrors him, and, in so doing, is destined to signify him. She speaks *lalangue*, but not that of the gods. It is only when she is away that the open heavens may thunder, that *lalangue* becomes poetic metaphysics. Hence, the mother gives rise to a world within the world, a world that is his, where he, by becoming an other, belongs, and which lies on *this* side of the rift between the world and the world. Beyond his world, lies the world, which is not his, but him, and which he is not.

If we are to regard *lalangue* as a language, the language of the gods, it is only insofar as the unimaginable stutters musically, or soundlessly, in the void beyond silence, thereby essentially functioning as a signifier that does not signify, but intimates. Hence, the difference between interpretation and divination. The interpretation of the signification of the unnameable belongs to the language of men; the divination of the intimations of the unimaginable belongs to the language of the gods.

Concerning the unnameable, which repeats in the void where emptiness and silence converge, and the language of men, we may say: *Yad'lun, il y a de l'Un*. There is something of the One.

Concerning the unimaginable, which repeats in the void where emptiness and darkness converge, and the language of the gods, we may say: *Yad'lzun, il y a de les uns*. There is something of the ones.

The essence of the language of the gods lies in this: the world speaks in counterpoint. *Lalangue*, the intimating language of appearance and disappearance, is the fugue of the gods.[55] The gods sing the subject, and the subject responds with the answer: the gods, as well as the subject, stutter the subject, but nothing stutters more than the fugue itself. In the *lalangue* of the gods, the answer, in being stuttered by the fugue, divines the intimations of the subject, in the form of an identity stated as difference. Just like a metaphor. Hence, the answer is a metaphor of the subject. Stated differently: the divination is a metaphor of the intimation. Accordingly, the *lalangue* of the gods, the fugue of the Others of the Other, divines its own intimations in metaphors based on identity under the guise of difference, just as the language of men, the discourse of the Other, interprets its own significations in metaphors based on difference under the guise of identity. The status of metaphor, stated in terms of identity and difference, determines the status of poetic logic as to its belonging to the language of the gods or to that of men.

What has man to divine in the encounter with a god? Owing to him not being mirrored by the unimaginable, the mirror throws his image into the unknown, into the void which keeps them apart – and there, they meet. The gods become familiar strangers. They are him and not him. They signify nothing, but, without him knowing it, they intimate him from *without*. Hence, what he has to divine, in the encounter with that which is most remote in his experience of the world, with that which he understands least of all, is himself. As in Vico's account of the emergence of the inconstant prophetic sea god Proteus:

> Just as children, looking in a mirror, will try to seize their own reflections, [the first men] thought from the various modifications of their own shapes and gestures that there must be a man in the water, forever changing into different shapes.[56]

In a paradoxical turn of events, the mirror makes of the irreducible indifference of the unimaginable a differential identity which does not reflect, an image without mirror image which the mirror created in the image of itself. Just like a metaphor. Thus, man, in speaking the language of the gods, divines intimations of himself, metaphorically, but not as himself, but as another, and, in so doing, is not an other, but himself and another.

Notes

1. Giambattista Vico, *La Scienza Nuova e Opere scelte* (Turin: UTET, 1966), s. 300. Slightly modified translation.
2. Jacques Lacan, *Seminar VII*, p. 121. "Is" instead of "are" in the translation.
3. Lacan, *Seminar VII*, pp. 121, 120.
4. Giambattista Vico, *New Science: Principles of the New Science Concerning the Common Nature of Nations*, trans. D. Marsh (London: Penguin, 2013), p. 144.
5. Vico, *New Science*, p. 140. This is Vico's attempt to explain the occurrence of giants, or Nephilim, in Genesis 6:1–4.
6. "Ignorance is the mother of wonder; and being ignorant of all things, the first people were amazed by everything. ... Whenever something aroused their feelings of wonder, they imagined its cause as a god. And at the same time, whatever aroused their wonder they endowed with a substantial being based on their own ideas". Vico, *New Science*, p. 144f.
7. Vico, *La Scienza Nuova*, p. 260.
8. Ibid., p. 330f.
9. Vico, *New Science*, p. 146.
10. Vico, *La Scienza Nuova*, p. 358f.
11. Vico, *New Science*, p. 147.
12. Giambattista Vico, *The New Science of Giambattista Vico*, trans. T. G. Bergin & M. H. Fisch (Ithaca/New York: Cornell University Press, 1948), pp. 114, 116f.
13. Vico, *New Science*, pp. 160, 158.
14. Ibid., p. 87.
15. Ibid., p. 214.
16. Ibid., p. 208.
17. Ibid., p. 223, 9.
18. Ibid., p. 142.

19 Giambattista Vico, *On the Most Ancient Wisdom of the Italians: Unearthed from the Origins of the Latin Language*, trans. L. M. Palmer (Ithaca/London: Cornell University Press, 1988), p. 46.
20 We know that Herder had been introduced to Vico's ideas, and, owing to the striking similarities of their conceptions, and to the reappearance of examples and arguments used by Vico, we must regard it as more than probable than Rousseau had heard of them too. In a footnote to *Of Grammatology*, Derrida writes:

> Bernard Gagnebin and Marcel Raymond have asked in connection with the *Essay of the Origin of Languages*, if Rousseau had not read the *Scienza Nuova* when he was Montaigu's secretary in Venice. … Cassier does not hesitate to affirm that Rousseau has 'summarized' in the *Essay* Vico's theories on Language.

> Jacques Derrida, *Of Grammatology*, trans. Gayatri Chakaravorty Spivak (Baltimore/London: Johns Hopkins University Press, 1997), p. 335, footnote 5.

21 Derrida himself affirms this: "Vico is one of the rare believers, if not the only believer, in the contemporaneity of origin between writing and speech". Derrida, *Of Grammatology*, p. 335, footnote 5.
22 See Samuel Beckett, "Dante… Bruno. Vico… Joyce", in Samuel Beckett, Marcel Brion, Frank Budgen, Stuart Gilbert, Eugene Jolas, Victor Llona, Robert McAlmon, Thomas McGreevy, Elliot Paul, John Rodker, Robert Sage, William Carlos Williams, G. V. K. Slingsby & Vladimir Dixon, *Our Exagmination Round His Factification for Incamination of Work in Progress* (New York: New Directions Books, 1972). Apart from the emphasis on the phonetic aspects of language, Vico also inspired Joyce to the extent that he wrote *Finnegan's Wake* in the model of *corsi e ricorsi storici*: in the book's very first sentence, which is famously a continuation of its last, Joyce makes a reference to this: "… brings us by a commodius vicus [i.e. Giambattista Vico, vicious circle] of recirculation back…". James Joyce, *Finnegan's Wake* (Ware: Wordsworth, 2012), s. 3. Or, as he puts it further on: "The Vico road goes round and round to meet where terms begin". Joyce, *Finnegan's Wake*, p. 452.
23 Jacques Lacan, *Seminar XXIII*, pp. 62–73.
24 I will immediately name the fundamental point where they differ. Although Vico could be said to anticipate the discovery of the dynamics and the language of the unconscious, he has no term whatsoever which would reflect the most fundamental concept of psychoanalysis, namely, the unconscious, and this is arguably conditioned by him lacking a conception of repression, or more generally, of defense mechanisms, resulting in him not conceiving of ignorance as a passion.
25 Sigmund Freud, "Constructions in Analysis", in *SE XXIII*, p. 259.
26 Vico, *New Science*, p. 93.
27 Which is to be taken quite literally concerning Freud, as is evident by his obsession about originary myths, as in the case of the primal scene, although its signification is also dependent on a retroactive causality.
28 Vico, *New Science*, p. 162, 24.
29 Ibid., p. 122.
30 Ibid., p. 125f.
31 Sigmund Freud, "Totem and Taboo", in *SE XIII*, p. 90.
32 Vico, *The New Science*, p. 129. Slightly modified translation.
33 Freud, "Totem and Taboo", p. 91. Slightly modified translation.
34 Freud, "Totem and Taboo", p. 65.
35 Ibid., p. 64. It is worth mentioning that both Vico and Freud perceive the origin of the belief in the soul derives from man's confrontation with death.
36 Freud, "Totem and Taboo", p. 92.
37 Sigmund Freud, "Psycho-Analytic Notes on an Autobiographical Account of a case of Paranoia (Dementia Paranoides)", in *SE XII*, p. 78.

38 Freud, "Psycho-Analytic Notes on an Autobiographical Account of a case of Paranoia (Dementia Paranoides)", p. 20.
39 This statement is evidently closer to Lacan than to Freud, since the latter gives repression a central role in his case study on Schreber.
40 Vico, *New Science*, p. 162.
41 Ibid.
42 Following Vico, we could go one step further than Lacan in equating not only displacement and condensation with metonymy and metaphor, respectively, but also secondary revision with irony.
43 Vico, *The New Science*, p. 70.
44 Giambattista Vico, *On the Most Ancient Wisdom of the Italians*, p. 39f.
45 Jacques Lacan, *Seminar XX*, p. 101, 138. Here, and elsewhere, I have chosen the original formulation *lalangue*, instead of llangue from the English translation.
46 Lacan, *Seminar XX*, p. 139.
47 Ibid.
48 Vico, *The New Science*, pp. 139, 136, 138.
49 Johann Gottfried Herder, "Essay on the Origin of Language", trans. Alexander Gode, in Jean-Jacques Rousseau & Johann Gottfried Herder, *On the Origin of Language* (Chicago/London: University of Chicago Press, 1986), pp. 98, 133.
50 This "forgetting" makes language *appear* as arbitrary. We could say that this forgetting is ultimately conditioned by this asymptotic movement, whereby synchrony and diachrony appear to be completely parallel. As Vico puts it:

> In general metaphor makes up the great body of the language among all nations. But the grammarians, encountering great numbers of words which give confused and indistinct ideas of things, and not knowing their origins, which had made them at first clear and distinct, have given peace to their ignorance by setting up the universal maxim that articulate human words have arbitrary significations.
> (Vico, *The New Science*, p. 132)

51 Beckett, "Dante... Bruno. Vico... Joyce", p. 5.
52 Vico, *The New Science*, p. 253.
53 Paraphrasing Pascal, and making reference to Lacan's negative meta-myth about *creatio ex nihilo*, we could say that the world is an infinite vase, the center of which is everywhere, the circumference nowhere.
54 This is why the speech of certain psychotics tends to be – often involuntarily – poetically beautiful, at times almost by default, for while the neurotic inhabits language, many psychotics live under the open sky, which, at times, speaks the intimating language of the gods, to which the psychotic responds with metaphors, which tend to be concrete and immediate – they are based on identity, and not difference. They are naively "true". As Vico puts it: "[the children of the nascent mankind created] by virtue of a wholly corporeal imagination. And because it was quite corporeal, they did it with marvelous sublimity". Vico, *The New Science*, p. 105.
55 A fugue commences with the first voice of the piece presenting what is referred to as the subject, the main theme of the fugue, after which the second voice enters and states what is called the answer, which, in general, is a transposition of the subject to a different key.
56 Vico, *The New Science*, p. 233.

Chapter 7
Ring/ring

It is but a lucky coincidence that the term "ring" has two different significations in the field of mathematics. The first one is "ring", or "circle", in topological knot theory, in which it signifies a closed loop, usually represented as a circle (or an ellipse of arbitrary eccentricity) in three-dimensional Euclidean space; the knot of greatest importance for Lacan's psychoanalysis is the "Borromean rings" (or knot, or link), consisting of three separate rings without interconnections, but which nonetheless hold together in such a way that the knot falls apart should any of the three rings be removed.

Figure 7.1 Borromean rings.

DOI: 10.4324/9781003278740-8

For Lacan, these rings represent the real, the symbolic, and the imaginary, which implies that the field of subjectivity is conceptualized as a topological knot whose constitutive components lack interconnections and fall apart would any of its three orders be subtracted.

However, the term "ring" may also refer to an *algebraic* ring, meaning a set with two operations, addition and multiplication (+ and •). This algebraic structure may be represented as (R, +, •) and is defined by the following criteria:

1 (R, +) is an Abelian group, that is:

   a R is closed under addition (+): if x and y are in R, then $z = x + y$ is also in R.
   b Addition is associative: for all x, y, and z in R, $(x + y) + z = x + (y + z)$.
   c There is an identity element *0* in R for which $x + 0 = x$ for all x in R.
   d Addition is invertible: for all x in R, there is a y in R for which $x + y = 0$. The inverse element can be written ($-x$), and the operation equivalent to addition with an inverse element is called subtraction (–).
   e Addition is commutative: for all x and y in R, $x + y = y + x$.

2 (R, •) is a semi-group, that is:

   a R is closed under multiplication (•): if x and y are elements in R, then $z = x • y$ is also an element in R.
   b Multiplication is associative: for all elements x, y, and z in R, $x • (y • z) = (x • y) • z$.

3 Multiplication (•) is distributive over addition (+): for all x, y, and z in R, $x • (y + z) = (x • y) + (x • z)$.

In addition to the fundamental criteria above, we may define the following subcategories:

4 A ring is unitary if there is an identity element *1* in R for which $x • 1 = x$ for all x in R.
5 A ring is a field if multiplication is invertible: for all x in R except *0*, there is an element y in R for which $x • y = 1$. The inverse element can be written ($1 / x$), and the inverse operation that is equivalent to multiplication with an inverse element is called division (/).

The operations addition and multiplication do not necessarily have the significations they have in ordinary arithmetic; however, it is easy to see that the set consisting of the whole numbers $\mathbf{Z} = \{...-3, -2, -1, 0, 1, 2, 3...\}$ is a ring (more specifically, a unitary ring, but not a field) under the operations addition and multiplication understood in the ordinary way.

I propose that we cease to think the real, the symbolic, and the imaginary as topological rings and instead as algebraic rings.[1] This means that we need to specify the elements and operations that define each of the rings:

1 ($\mathcal{S}$, μ, M) is a ring which we name the symbolic order ($\mathcal{S}$) consisting of signifiers (S) obeying the operations metonymy (μ) and metaphor (M).

   a The metonymic operation (μ) on two successive signifiers results in a third signifier preserving the successive order. Metonymy may be regarded as an operation that generates a successively ordered chain of signifiers whose elements are contiguous with one another.

   b The metonymic operation is invertible: the inverse operation ($μ^{-1}$) on two successive signifiers results in a third signifier that inverts the successive order. We name this inverse operation negation (in Freud's and Lacan's sense of the term) which may be regarded as an operation that switches direction on a successively ordered chain of signifiers.

   c The metaphoric operation (M) on two successive signifiers results in a third signifier that replaces one of the elements it operates upon and thus substitutes one signifier in a successively ordered chain of signifiers.[2]

   d The metaphoric operation is invertible: the inverse operation (M^{-1}) on two successive signifiers results in a third signifier that replaces one of the elements it operates upon. We name this inverse operation repression (in Freud's and Lacan's sense of the term).[3]

2 ($\mathcal{I}$, σ, Σ) is a ring which we name the imaginary order ($\mathcal{I}$) consisting of images (i) obeying the operations synthesis (σ) and superposition (Σ).

   a The synthesizing operation (σ) on two images generates a third image by combining the images it operates upon. The synthesizing function may be regarded as an operation that unites different images, thus creating a whole (in Klein's sense of the term).

   b The synthesizing operation is invertible: the inverse operation ($σ^{-1}$) on a synthesized image and one of its part images subtracts the latter from the former, thus resulting in the remaining part image. The inverse function may be regarded as an operation that separates part images, thus hindering or reversing the formation of a whole. We name this inverse operation splitting (in Klein's sense of the term).

   c The superimposing operation (Σ) on two images results in a third image by layering them. Superposition may be regarded (as in wave physics) as an operation amplifying similarities (constructive interference) and de-amplifying differences (destructive interference) between the superimposed images, thus generating an abstraction enabling the two images to resemble (in Plato's sense of the term) each other.

   d The superimposing operation is invertible: the inverse operation ($Σ^{-1}$) on an abstract image and a concrete image results in another concrete image that is dissociated from the abstraction that makes it similar to the former concrete image. Thus, the inverse operation amplifies differences and de-amplifies similarities between two concrete images, resulting in one of them veiling the other as well as their abstract affinity. We name this inverse operation disavowal (in Freud's sense of the term), which gives rise to a veiling image (for example, fetish or phobia in Freud's sense of these terms).

3 ($\mathcal{R}$, δ, Δ) is a ring which we name the real order ($\mathcal{R}$) consisting of ex-sisting elements (r) obeying the operations fusion (δ) and fission (Δ). The real elements may also be regarded as beta-elements (in Bion's sense of the term).

   a The fusing operation (δ) on two beta-elements results in a third beta-element by melding them. Fusion may be regarded as the merging of real elements, resulting in their undifferentiated unification.
   b The fissioning operation (Δ) on a fused beta-element and one of its parts tears the latter apart from the former, thus resulting in the other beta-element that remains. Fission may be regarded as the decomposition of real elements, resulting in their disintegration and subsequent dispersion. Fission and fusion are each other's inverses.

We may regard $\mathcal{R}$, $\mathcal{S}$, and $\mathcal{J}$ as three separate orders understood as algebraic rings whose operations act *only* within their respective ring. This implies that symbolic, imaginary, and real operations act only upon elements in their respective orders and that their end products cannot escape them. Thus, nothing makes it necessary for there to exist instances linking elements from different orders to each other. This may be interpreted as holding that there necessarily is a possibility of there being absences of instances serving to regulate the interaction between the different rings, that is, between elements belonging to separate orders. We may topically represent the spaces separating the orders as voids and algebraically represent these voids as Ø. Thus, there is Ø between $\mathcal{R}$ and $\mathcal{S}$, $\mathcal{R}$ and $\mathcal{J}$, $\mathcal{S}$ and $\mathcal{J}$, and in the central space between $\mathcal{R}$, $\mathcal{S}$, and $\mathcal{J}$. Hence, we may understand Ø not only as a space where the rings drift apart, or diverge, but also as a venue where elements from different rings without interconnections *may* encounter, or converge, by coincidence, that is to say without their interaction being determined or regulated by any order or necessity. Furthermore, we may postulate that, given that favorable conditions are at hand, instances *may* consolidate where the orders diverge, and that these instances *may* fulfill the function of regulating the interaction between elements residing in separate rings, and that these instances are organized in and around the central void Ø. Let us name these hypothetical instances: α signifies any instance situated at the disjunction of the real and the imaginary; β signifies any instance situated at the disjunction of the symbolic and the imaginary; γ signifies any instance situated at the disjunction of the symbolic and the real. Hence, we may algebraically represent the field of subjectivity as [α, β, γ], given that we let α, β, or γ be equal to Ø, which would signify that no instance has been consolidated at the disjunction of the rings in question; and topically represent this with an image that only superficially corresponds to Lacan's Borromean rings:

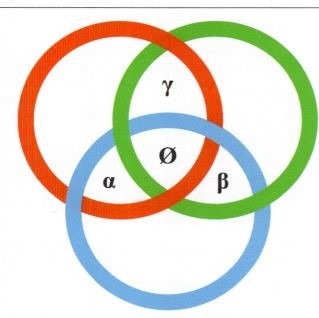

Figure 7.2 Topical representation of the field of subjectivity.

α, β, and γ may be understood as follows:

1 α signifies any instance localized in the void where the imaginary and the real diverge. Such an instance would fulfill the function to connect, differentiate, and regulate interactions between beta-element and image, ex-sistence and consistency, sense impression and fantasy, *jouissance* and narcissism, formlessness and whole. The absence of such an instance would result in repeated and unforeseeable collisions between the rings, which would imply that the real incessantly invades the imaginary and hinders the image from neutralizing the traumatic and unbearable effects of the beta-elements, as well as the stabilization of consistency. The consolidation of α is equivalent to a transition from a psychical functioning dominated by overwhelming disorder into one characterized by imaginary consistency, which roughly corresponds to the constitution of the alpha-function (Bion), the transition from the paranoid-schizoid to the depressive position (Klein), and the constitution of the ideal ego in the mirror stage (Lacan).[4] This also results in the stabilization of primary narcissism (in Freud's and Lacan's sense of the term). The instance normally functioning as α is the empty mirror; let us designate it with the algebraic symbol i(Ø). The primary effects of the mirror stage: the mirror, consistency, the ideal ego, and primary narcissism.
2 β signifies any instance localized in the void where the imaginary and the symbolic diverge. Such an instance would fulfill the function to connect, differentiate, and regulate interactions between the fields of the ego and the Other;

between word and image, signifier and signified, law and narcissism, lack and consistency, difference and resemblance. The absence of such an instance would result in the dissolution of the sign understood (in Saussure's sense of the term) as the unity of the signifier and the signified, whose immediate effect would thus be the absence of stabilized meaning. This would also imply that the ego, understood (in Lacan's sense of the term) as an imaginary accretion of specular identifications, lacks an anchoring point in the symbolic, which leaves narcissism without a regulating point of reference in the field of the Other with respect to its demands, prohibitions, norms, conventions, limits. The consolidation of β is equivalent to a transition from primary narcissism and identification to secondary narcissism and identification (in Freud's and Lacan's senses of these terms), that is, that the position of the ego in the imaginary goes from being determined primarily by the mirror image to being determined primarily by the ego ideal, which, by anchoring the ego in the symbolic, would stabilize the identity of the subject. The instance normally functioning as β is the ego ideal; we follow Lacan and designate it with the algebraic symbol I(A). This transition roughly corresponds to some of the aspects of the process of alienation-separation in Lacan's sense of these terms, and for the sake of clarity, I will refer to the process of consolidation of the ego ideal as "symbolic alienation". The primary effects of symbolic alienation: ego ideal, meaning, secondary narcissism, and stabilized identity.

3   γ signifies any instance localized in the void where the symbolic and the real diverge. Such an instance would fulfill the function to connect, differentiate, and regulate interactions between *jouissance* and law, sexuality and limit, lust and norm, drive and the Other. The absence of such an instance would result in *jouissance* incessantly invading the symbolic without its limits being able to neutralize it, resulting in *jouissance* to periodically overwhelm it. This would imply that the law has not become operative with respect to *jouissance*, that is, that sexuality is transgressive, and that sexuality has not been bound by limits anchored in linguistic structures. This transition roughly corresponds to castration (in Lacan's sense of the term). The instance normally functioning as γ is the phallic function, that is, a signifying structure that introduces the sexual difference by the institution of the symbolic phallus; we follow Lacan and designate the phallic function with the algebraic symbol Φ. The primary effects of castration: phallic function, phallic *jouissance*, and sexual difference.

[α, β, γ] give rise to exactly eight different configurations depending on whether α, β, and γ are consolidated or not, and we may equate each of these configurations with a clinical structure.[5] These are the following:

1   [Ø, β, γ]. This clinical structure is defined by the absence of consolidated mirror, that is, by α = Ø. This means that there is no consolidated instance regulating the interaction between the real and the imaginary, which implies that the subject has not finalized the mirror stage. The absence of consolidated α means first and foremost that the mirror does not function, that consistency has not

been stabilized, and that the real has not been neutralized. This configuration defines the *autistic* structure. Dependent on whether β and γ have been consolidated or not, four possibilities arise which can be seen as four variations of the autistic structure, in that they have in common that α = Ø. [Ø, Ø, Ø] may be regarded as the most extreme form of autism ("psychotic autism") characterized by language not being inscribed as an order in its own right with regulating effects with respect to the real; [Ø, I(A), Φ] may, on the contrary, be seen as its "mildest" version, approximating the symptomatology sometimes referred to as "Asperger's" (or "neurotic autism"). A significant part of the secondary symptoms of autism may be grasped as attempts to, through real repetition or symbolic rigidity, establish a pseudo-consistency compensating for the lacking imaginary consistency that follows from the malfunctioning of the mirror.

2 [i(Ø), Ø, Ø]. This clinical structure is defined by the presence of the mirror and the absence of consolidated ego ideal and phallic function, that is, by α = i(Ø), β = Ø, and γ = Ø, which means that the subject has finalized the mirror stage but neither symbolic alienation nor castration, which implies that the symbolic order has not been inscribed as a field in its own right, and that the frail unity of the real and the imaginary established by the mirror lacks anchorage in it. This configuration corresponds to Lacan's *psychotic* structure, and does not deviate significantly from his understanding of it.

3 [i(Ø), I(A), Ø]. This clinical structure is defined by the presence of the mirror and the ego ideal and the absence of consolidated phallic function, that is, by α = i(Ø), β = I(A), and γ = Ø, which means that the subject has undergone the mirror stage and symbolic alienation but not finalized castration, which implies that the sexual difference has not been recognized, and that the law has not been instituted with respect to *jouissance*. This configuration corresponds to Lacan's *perverse* structure, and does not deviate significantly from his understanding of it.

4 [i(Ø), I(A), Φ]. This clinical structure is defined by the presence of the mirror, the ego ideal, and the phallic function, that is, by α = i(Ø), β = I(A), and γ = Φ, which means that the subject has finalized the mirror stage, symbolic alienation, and castration. This configuration corresponds to Lacan's *neurotic* structure, and does not deviate significantly from his understanding of it.

5 [i(Ø), Ø, Φ]. This clinical structure is defined by the presence of the mirror and the phallic function and the absence of consolidated ego ideal, that is, by α = i(Ø), β = Ø, and γ = Φ, which means that the subject has undergone the mirror stage and castration but not finalized symbolic alienation. The absence of consolidated β means first and foremost that ideals do not function, that meaning has not been stabilized, and that the identity has not been consolidated. This state defines the clinical structure roughly corresponding to Kernberg's *borderline* personality organization and Kohut's *narcissistic* personality disorder. The non-consolidation of the ego ideal implies a propensity for primary narcissism and identification, while the concomitant dissolution of the sign results in what may be described as symbolic and imaginary disorder, as well as empty speech detached from the vividness of images.

From the formalization above, we can derive that there necessarily exists exactly eight distinct clinical structures (four of which are to be understood as variations of one overarching structure) – there can be no more or less. These are autism, psychosis, perversion, borderline, and neurosis, which are understood as proceeding from (in the normal case) the mirror, the ego ideal, and the phallic function and their contingent emergence in the void Ø. We may regard Ø as a fundamentally real void that is not an effect of language, and name it *emptiness*. Emptiness extends and borders the rings and fills their inner cavities; we may define the regions of emptiness that fill symbolic voids as *silence* and the regions of emptiness that fill imaginary voids as *darkness*. We may see that emptiness, darkness, and silence converge in the center of the field of subjectivity – the space where the real, the imaginary, and the symbolic diverge – this is the nature of the unconscious. We may conjecture that the phallic function relegates elements in the space where the symbolic and the real diverge to the void where silence and emptiness converge; that the ego ideal relegates elements in the space where the symbolic and the imaginary diverge to the void where silence and darkness converge; that the mirror relegates elements in the space where the imaginary and the real diverge to void where darkness and emptiness converge. We may also note that the region of the field of subjectivity where darkness and emptiness converge constitutes a void that is strictly speaking *outside* and thus completely independent of language. In this void resides not the unnamable, but the *unimaginable*: the mysterious, the vertiginous, the horrifying, the sublime – beyond silence, in solitude within, without the absence of the Other.[6]

Notes

1. I will use the term "ring", although the sets in question are not rings in the strict sense of the word, since all criteria are not fulfilled for all sets. The mathematical category "ring-like" would strictly speaking be more adequate.
2. Here, I clearly use the term "metaphor" in Lacan's sense of the word, and not Vico's.
3. Metaphor and repression are obviously identical, implying that repression is metaphorical.
4. These references to developmental stages are consciously made vague and only for the sake of clarity. They should not be interpreted as implying any form of linear or teleological temporality, order, or necessity.
5. There is no definitive way of establishing the clinical structures outlined below in any particular case, owing to there being no definitive way of determining if consolidated instances are "present" or "absent", for the simple reason that it is a question not of absolute binarity, but of relative stability. Moreover, although these instances are situated in the voids between the rings, they do not simply erase or fill them; the voids are unsaturable, implying the impossibility of complete consolidation or stabilization. Lastly, the approximate non-consolidation or malfunctioning of any instance will inevitable significantly disturb the functioning of the others, as is evident when considering identity and narcissism in perversion, and sexuality and limits in the borderline structure.
6. This mathematization of psychoanalytic metapsychology may be conceived as a concatenation of two essentially distinct and thus relatively independent aspects: first, the rethinking of the three orders as algebraic rings; second, the conceptualization of the field of subjectivity and the clinical structures in terms of the separation of the three orders understood as converging voids. It should be clear for the reader that these two aspects have radically different statuses in relation to that which I have hitherto proposed in the course of this book. The topical representation of the field of subjectivity is much more essential than the algebraic re-conceptualization of the rings.

Chapter 8

From Beyond the Real

To conclude, I find it necessary to dwell upon some philosophical problems which what I have hitherto put forward inevitably raises. The most essential ones, which I believe only partially may be adequately answered psychoanalytically, are the following: *how* can there be an independent void in the real, and *why* is there one? Here, I will present some philosophical reflections, proceeding from which you could argue that it cannot possibly be otherwise.

Thus, here follows three philosophical sections, before I return, as briefly and concise as possible, to the topic of the status of rings and voids in psychoanalytic theory.

Clinamen

The concept *clinamen* was coined during the first century BC by the Roman poet Titus Lucretius Carus in the epic didactic poem *De rerum natura* (*On the Nature of Things*), which is generally perceived as the most detailed exposition of Epicurean philosophy that remains from Antiquity. Just as in the case of his Greek master, Lucretius proceeded from the conception of the universe as an endless void encompassing an infinite amount of aimlessly drifting atoms which, by clashing in this emptiness, enter into constellations which enter into constellations which enter into constellations which build up a world amongst an infinite amount of worlds that coalesce and drift apart in an eternal all-encompassing vacuum. Everything that exists, including human beings and their souls, is a product of non-necessary encounters between atoms falling in the abyss.

The encounters of the atoms in the void may be grasped under the term "contingency", from Latin *contingere*, from *cum-* ("together") and *tangere* ("touch"): "to touch each other", "to come into contact with each another", "to encounter". In modal logic, this term signifies a statement which is neither necessarily true nor false, that is, which *may* but does not *need* to be true. A contingent event *may* but does not *need* to take place: it *occurs* (*ob-*, "towards", and *curro*: "run into", "meet") by *coincidence* (*co-*, "together"; *in*, "into"; *cadere*, "to fall": "fall towards each other"). Encounters necessarily *take place* by co-incidence.

DOI: 10.4324/9781003278740-9

Epicure's heretic physics denies the world any overarching meaning, order, goal, stability, permanence, necessity; Lucretius's term *clinamen* constitutes the culmination of its radicalism. In the second book of *De rerum natura*, we read:

> When first-bodies are being carried downwards straight through the void by their own weight, at times quite undetermined and at undetermined places they push a little from their path: yet only just so much as you could call a change of trend. But if they were not used to swerve, all things would fall downwards through the deep void like drops of rain, nor could collision come to be, nor a blow brought to pass for the first-beginnings: so nature would never have brought aught to being.[1]
>
> (II. 217–224)

Lucretius draws the image of the atomic rain, of a cascade of solitary particles tumbling in parallel through the void. Were it not the case that they spontaneously deviate from their straight path, "swerve a little; yet not more than the very least",[2] no encounter would have taken place and nothing would have come into existence. It is only the insignificant and incalculable deviation that may "bring about the blows, which make diverse the movements, by which nature carries things on" (II. 241–242).[3] The beginning of the world is thus thought of as an original collision between adjacent elements generating a chain reaction propagating through the laminar atomic flow giving rise to an increasingly complex jumble of particles. But even more original than the first encounter is "the tiny swerve (*clinamen*) of the first-beginnings at no determined place and at no determined time" (II. 292–293).[4] What does *clinamen* signify? In the verses that precede the formulation, Lucretius sometimes makes use of the term *inclinare*, but above all *declinare*, from *clino*, "I lean", "I bend". The prefixes *de-* and *in-* imply that the slope is determined negatively, in Lucretius's case in relation to the straight line. *Declinare* means to *de-cline*, to "bend off", to *de-viate* from the line (*de via*, "off the road"). In *clinamen*, the negative prefixes are subtracted – we could speak of a pure "clination" or "viation". It is a term that is positively determined, but which nonetheless signifies "something" which is neither positive nor negative, and, furthermore, which seems unimaginable owing to our intuition being bound to the Euclidean representation of the straight line. *Clinamen* is a sudden infinitesimal perturbation that takes place without any reason whatsoever, while simultaneously being able to "break through the decrees of faith, so that cause may not follow cause from infinite time" (II. 254–255);[5] an ungraspable, unpredictable, insignificant occurrence in space and time which violates every rational necessity; a cause without cause for the spontaneous decomposition, transformation, emergence of everything that is – and solely responsible for the existence of the world.

If there is a term in contemporary vocabulary that approximates the nature of *clinamen*, it is doubtless "chance". The problem lays in thinking this chance, which derives from Latin *casus*, *cadere*, which at the same time means "to fall" and "to occur". The fact that the etymologic roots of chance converge with the

Epicurean image of contingency enables us to discern the difficulties in conceptually differentiating between coincidence and chance; it is as if contingency only asymptotically approaches unthinkable chance. The representation of chance as roll of the dice, as aleatory (*alea*, "dice"), testifies of this: the freedom of chance is limited by the fact that the dice has a determined amount of faces, and that its rotation along the parabola is nevertheless dictated by the laws of physics. Chance cannot liberate itself from coincidence in thought; it is not possible to exemplify the clination. "Every thought emits a throw of the dice" (Mallarmé) betrays chance; in chance, the dice is thrown away.

Metaontics

The problem with *clinamen* is that it, by definition, is deeply disturbing, and that it disturbs from the deep, and in the deep. This, in essence, is due to it being irremediably *ontic* (in a Greek and not a Heideggerian sense), which is to say that it is valid for "that which is", and that it, by definition, is "not more than the very least", localized on the world's most microscopic scale, but that it nonetheless is operative on all of its levels – including that of thought. Everything is subordinated to the omnipotence of the pathetic clination, for the simple reason that it can create and transform and destroy everything that is at any given time and without any reason whatsoever. Given that a theory affirms the superiority of the negligible clination that it was granted in *De rerum natura*, its effects must also make themselves felt on this very theory. These implications go far beyond the assertion of the impotence of language in relation to its object, and beyond the meta-linguistic affirmation of the instability and incompleteness of language, and its lacking capacity to grasp and reflect upon itself. The clination operates in language, on language, from language, beyond language – but most importantly *outside* and thus completely *independent* of language. The first among all of the steps (we will soon go one step further than Lucretius) that follows from seriously affirming *clinamen* is to affirm *nature* and that language is a part of nature. This means neither that language is "natural", nor that it has no field of its own within nature, but only that language – just like the word and the human being – is a *thing* that is subordinated to the fundamental determinants of nature. This is to affirm that language is subordinated to the ontic – that language in effect is not only inscribed within the ontic but also that it itself *is* ontic. This implies that language, for reasons of principle, *must* give the ontic primacy over thought as such, and thus also over the thought about the ontic – that is, about nature – in other words, *physics*, and that physics, in turn, is given primacy over language, *from the perspective of language*.

A trivial example: language needs to consider the implications of the fact that everything will perish. It is worth thinking about. What will be of Hegel's dialectic when stars detonate, when all things dissipate? What will be of Badiou's eternity when the trace of mankind in the world is erased far after extinction? If thought and man and life are things, and the world approximates a state where things are no more, what will be of every ontology which depends on thought, man, life, things? The end of the world confronts philosophy with the great questions. Does time survive history, inscription, the subject, Da-sein? That is: what is time? What outlives things? That is: what is not a thing? When language is no more, what is there? Which leads us to the questions of questions: does mathematics outlive the thinker? That is: is the ontic mathematical or is mathematics ontic? That is: what is mathematics? What is "there"? What is "is"? What is "there is"?

Let us for the sake of simplicity imagine that the field of ontology consists of three fundamental dimension which we, at least preliminarily and in thought, may regard as separated (this is the question): ὄντος, λόγος, μάθημα. The ontic, language, mathematics. The rifts separating the dimensions from each other, the borderlands of the ontological domains, we may allocate to three different branches of philosophy. The borderland of the ontic and mathematics, philosophy has rightly been forced to give up: physics, the mathematical science of nature. The borderland of language and mathematics: logic. The borderland of language and the ontic: *metaontics*.

Metaontics: philosophy of things. Its first postulate: the world is all that is. Language is ontic – hence meta-ontic, logo-ontic, philontosophy. The word is a region of the world, language is a thing that is. *Ethics*, Book II, Axiom II: *homo cogitat*.

This first, empty, trivial postulate – which evidently is formulated to contradict the logical equivalent of Wittgenstein – needs to be complemented by a linguistic statement that specifies it proceeding from the mathematical thought about the ontic, physics. This "choice" is not "arbitrary" in the linguistic sense, but occasional, in a double sense: non-permanent, and the result of a contingent encounter between elements from radically different domains in thought (that is, in the world), which, for reasons which ultimately do not let themselves be specified, fall in direction of one another.

The leading and most fruitful contemporary theory about the nature of nature is *quantum field theory* – here *clinamen* returns. It is reasonable for the time being to grant it a privileged status as to the most fundamental determinants of the ontic. This is not in place, or for that sake doable, to here summarize or contextualize quantum field theory; it is enough for our purposes to immediately formulate some of its principal statements in a clear and concise philosophical language. Some fundamental philosophical theses:

1 The world is all that is;
2 all that is is a field;
3 the field consists of discrete excitations (elementary particles) that are created and annihilated at no determined place and at no determined time;
4 excitations propagate through the field and encounter and enter into constellations (things) at times quite undetermined and at undetermined places; constellations propagate through the field and encounter and dissolve and enter into further constellations at times quite undetermined and at undetermined places;
5 et cetera.

Comments on 1–6:

1 the first postulate;
2 the second postulate, the "choice" of field theory, more specifically, quantum field theory (unlike, for example, Epicurean or Newtonian physics, or the Greek, Egyptian, Sumerian, or Abrahamitic field myths: Χάος, Nun, Tiamat, tohu wa-bohu);
3 the fundamental view of quantum field theory on the relation between field and particle. He who wishes to visualize the quantum field may picture himself an undulating, chaotic ocean, where each wave represents a discrete excitation, an elementary particle, and where the aleatory rise and fall of the wave represents the creation and annihilation of the particle in question. The field generates and extinguishes the constituents of things, incessantly and for no reason whatsoever, by chance. Only the field is indestructible. Back to ἄπειρον, back to Λήθη. "At no determined place and at no determined time" refers to the aleatory, uncertain, ghostlike causality of *clinamen*, characteristic of the effectivity of quantum mechanics: the primary chaos of the field. The omnipotence of the clination has here been extended: it does possess not only the power to change the courses of events of already existing, indestructible elements (the atoms of Leucippus) but also the power to create and annihilate the most fundamental constituents of things (elementary particles);
4 on the emergence of things, for example, proton, word, language, human, earth. "Propagate, encounter, enter, dissolve", "at times quite undetermined and at undetermined places": the secondary contingency of the field;
5 all that is is a chaotic field that creates and annihilates elementary particles by chance which form things by coincidence constructed through a finite series of repetitions within the limits of 3–4. If there is any necessity in the world, it is tertiary and approximate and logically subordinated to secondary contingency which, in so far as there is any contingency in the world, is secondary and approximate and logically subordinated to primary chance. Contingency is a deviation from chance and emerges from chaos owing to *clinamen*; necessity is a deviation from contingency and emerges from disorder owing to encounters. The line is a deviation from the clination and not vice versa. The eventual insignificance of chance or contingency for macroscopic things is conditioned by statistical effects of repetitions of 3–4, that is, by 5. 5 is, in the last instance, a result of 3–4; many ontologies omit 1–3, as if the field did not exist – to kill Great Pan again.

Everything emerges from and returns to the field.

On the Nature of Things

Proceeding from these reflections, we may distinguish between three different kinds of things corresponding to three different forms of domains, which we may understand analogically from the perspective of field theory, atomism, and mechanics: excitations of fields, elements in space, constituents of structures. The dynamics peculiar to these things and domains are governed by three different causal modalities: chance, contingency, and necessity; and their macroscopic and microscopic approximative realizations, respectively, are chaos and *clinamen*, disorder and encounter, order and action; and the metric under which they fall are existence, distance, and difference.

In the field, there is no void, for the void of the world is not empty. The ocean is full, the world is full, full of undulations, waves, torrents. There is nothing but the field, a field which, in itself, is nothing but waves upon waves, chaotically emerging and disappearing by chance amongst themselves – but, from the depth of the immense sum of the waves of the field, which is all there is, singular waves stand out, discrete excitations come into existence, towering, as solitary elements. Between the crests of the waves, there is distance, and, summing up the distances between the waves, space emerges, a space in which waves propagate independently of each other, linearly, in a state of general disorder. Hence, when excitations emerge from the field, space, and the elements which populate it, come into existence simultaneously. If there are elements, there is space, and there can be no space without elements, and, insofar as the field does not annihilate these elements by chance, they cannot but propagate linearly in a state of disorder. Space, elements, and disorder are equiprimordial. None of them can be without the others. Thus, the elements, which come into existence by chance, when propagating linearly in space independently of each other, encounter by coincidence, like atoms in the infinite void. They fall and they meet, and, in so doing, they may, or may not, form torrents, perpetually relating to each other, and, through each other, to themselves, circularly. They act upon one another, incessantly, and without this incessant reciprocal action, which makes them whirl and whirl, they fall apart, return to space as distinct elements, propagating independently of each other, again. But if their action happens to keep them together, the perpetually interrelating elements become the constituents of a torrent, which, by interiorizing elements, perpetuates its own existence, relates to itself, mediately, through its constituents. A structure comes to be, an order of interrelated, differentiated constituents, following the necessity of the reproductive motion of the vortex. Thus, structure, constituents, and order are equiprimordial. Nevertheless, in the very center of the torrent, which emerged by coincidence in space, there are no constituents, only a space falling down into the

Table 8.1 Modalities of things

Domain	Field	Space	Structure
Thing	Excitation	Element	Constituent
Causal modality	Chance	Contingency	Necessity
Macroscopic realization	Chaos	Disorder	Order
Microscopic realization	*Clinamen*	Encounter	Action
Metric	Existence	Distance	Difference
Geometry	Singularity	Linearity	Circularity
Theory	Field theory	Atomism	Mechanics

depth of the field. There, excitations emerge by chance, and elements propagate by coincidence; there, its constituents return to space contingently, rendering them elements once more, or, by being annihilated by the field by chance, return to the depth of the field. Thus, space is a void that emerges from chaotic plenitude, and lies at the heart of every ordered structure.[6] In-between field and structure, there is space; in-between excitations and constituents, there are elements; in-between chance and necessity, there is contingency; in-between chaos and order, there is disorder; in-between *clinamen* and action, there are encounters; in-between existence and difference, there is distance; in between singularity and circularity, there is linearity – or, analogically stated in terms of different levels of abstraction of theoretical physics: in-between field theory and mechanics, there is atomism.

Rings and Voids

It is time to return to the rings and voids of the field of subjectivity – the real, the imaginary, and the symbolic.[7]

They are things. Hence, they consist of things: beta-elements, images, and signifiers.

They are things. Hence, they are governed by necessity.

The real is unitary, its constituents do not relate. The unitary necessity of the real belongs to the order of repetition.

The imaginary is dyadic, each constituent relate to its other. The dyadic necessity of the imaginary belongs to the order of reflection.

The symbolic is triadic, its constituents relate to each other. The triadic necessity of the symbolic belongs to the order of reference.

They are things. Hence, they carry spaces within themselves. In these spaces, there are no things. There are voids: emptiness, darkness, silence.

They are things. Hence, rings and voids are equiprimordial. One cannot exist without the other. They come to be, and cease to be, together. They are full and empty, by definition.

They are things. Hence, in the voids which they carry within themselves, there is no order, no necessity. There is disorder, contingency. In emptiness, the real does

Table 8.2 Modalities of rings

Ring	Real	Imaginary	Symbolic
Constituents	Beta-element	Image	Signifier
Space	Emptiness	Darkness	Silence
Arithmetic	Unitary	Dyadic	Triadic
Order	Repetition	Reflection	Reference
Addition	Fusion	Synthesis	Metonymy
Additive inverse	Fission	Splitting	Negation
Multiplication	Fission	Superposition	Metaphor
Multiplicative inverse	Fusion	Disavowal	Repression

not repeat. In darkness, the imaginary does not reflect. In silence, the symbolic does not refer. They fall. In these voids, encounters take place, by definition.

What is the nature of the unconscious? It is the field of the field of subjectivity. In this field, there is no order or disorder, no necessity or contingency. There is, from the perspective of rings, only chaos, chance. It is what space descends towards. It is what that which is emerges from. From this field, singular, non-existent things come into existence, from afar, like bolts of lightning.

The End of Psychoanalysis

Is there, below the non-existence that lies buried within the field of subjectivity, an existence that is even more existent than existence itself?

What lies beyond that which we cannot see? The field, the One, nature, mathematics, oblivion, chaos, being, nothing?

Of this, psychoanalysis has nothing to say. Thereof, it must be silent. This is the outer edge of psychoanalysis. If there is something beyond, it begins where psychoanalysis ends.

Notes

1. Lucretius, *On the Nature of Things*, trans. Cyril Bailey (Oxford: Clarendon Press, 1948), p. 72. "At undetermined spots" in Bailey's translation.
2. Lucretius, *On the Nature of Things*, p. 73.
3. Ibid.
4. Lucretius, *On the Nature of Things*, p. 75. "In no determined direction of place" in Bailey's translation.
5. Lucretius, *On the Nature of Things*, p. 74f.
6. Hence, we may distinguish between three forms of temporality: those of fields, spaces, and structures. This is what enables us to speak of a "before" the time peculiar to structure. In psychoanalytic terms: of the symbolic. Although no structure may truly go beyond its own limits, there is a temporality peculiar to space and disorder, that is, a time wherein structure emerges contingently through *encounters*. This is a corollary to this philosophy of things. This is why I have earlier frequently used terms such as "may, or may not". This also avoids developmental dead-ends; it is inherently anti-linear and anti-"teleological" – but it is also anti-"structuralist". In short, concerning the coincidental emergence of a new structure, there is no necessity. The elements which, after contingent encounters in space, become constituents of a structure, are "already" there, that is, "elsewhere" in the field of subjectivity. Hence, it would be wholly incorrect to speak of transcendence: concerning structure and elements, there is no true "beyond", only a radical "elsewhere"; distance, space, void. It would, however, not be wholly inadequate to speak of a "beyond" of the field of subjectivity. This "beyond" would be its field, that is, that from which hitherto non-existent excitations come to be. This would amount to an intrusion of the radically new. This, however, is not a true "beyond" either, since the world is all that is, and the field of subjectivity, including its field, is but a thing within it. From another level of abstraction, which would not be properly psychoanalytic, that which is perceived as the field of the field of subjectivity would appear under another modality. Stated differently: there is no true beyond in or of the world.
7. I wish to underline that there is no necessary connection between that which I speak of as things and my conceptualization of the three orders as rings. The order of the structure determines the nature of the thing, and there is no need to conceptualize the order or operations of a structure mathematically.

References

Arabi, I. M., *The Bezels of Wisdom*, trans. R. W. J. Austin. Mahwah: Paulist Press, 1980.
Arabi, I. M., *The Seals of Wisdom*. Santa Barbara: Concord Grove Press, 1983.
Beckett, S. "Dante… Bruno. Vico… Joyce." In Beckett, S., Brion, M., Budgen, F., Gilbert, S., Jolas, E., Llona, V., McAlmon, R., McGreevy, T., Paul, E., Rodker, J., Sage, R., Williams, W. C., Slingsby, G. V. K., & Dixon, V., *Our Exagmination Round His Factification for Incamination of Work in Progress*. New York: New Directions Books, 1972.
Bion, W. R., *Attention and Interpretation*. London/New York: Karnac, 2007.
Bion, W. R., *Two Papers: The Grid and Caesura*. London: Karnac, 2007.
Bollas, C., *The Shadow of the Object: Psychoanalysis of the Unthought Known*. New York/London: Routledge, 2018.
Derrida, J., *Of Grammatology*, trans. G. C. Spivak. Baltimore/London: Johns Hopkins University Press, 1997.
Einstein, A., *The Collected Papers of Albert Einstein. Volume 7. The Berlin Years: Writings 1918–1921*, trans. A. Engel. Princeton/Oxford: Princeton University Press, 2002.
Ekelöf, G., *Samlade dikter I*. Stockholm: Atlantis, 2016.
Freud, S., *The Standard Edition of the Complete Psychological Works of Sigmund Freud, Volume V (1900–1901): The Interpretation of Dreams (Second Part)* and *On Dreams*, trans. J. Strachey. London: Hoghart Press, 1953.
Freud, S., *The Standard Edition of the Complete Psychological Works of Sigmund Freud Volume XII (1911–1913): The Case of Schreber, Papers on Technique* and *Other Works*, trans. J. Strachey. London: Hoghart Press, 1958.
Freud, S., *The Standard Edition of the Complete Psychological Works of Sigmund Freud Volume XIII (1913–1914): Totem and Taboo* and *Other Works*, trans. J. Strachey. London: Hoghart Press, 1955.
Freud, S., *The Standard Edition of the Complete Psychological Works of Sigmund Freud Volume XIV (1914–1916): On the History of the Psycho-Analytic Movement, Papers on Metapsychology* and *Other Works*, trans. J. Strachey. London: Hoghart Press, 1957.
Freud, S., *The Standard Edition of the Complete Psychological Works of Sigmund Freud Volume XVII (1917–1919): An Infantile Neurosis* and *Other Works*, trans. J. Strachey. London: Hoghart Press, 1955.
Freud, S., *The Standard Edition of the Complete Psychological Works of Sigmund Freud Volume XIX (1923–1925): The Ego and the Id* and *Other Works*, trans. J. Strachey. London: Hoghart Press, 1961.
Freud, S., *The Standard Edition of the Complete Psychological Works of Sigmund Freud Volume XX (1925–1926): An Autobiographical Study, Inhibitions, Symptoms and Anxiety,*

The Question of Lay Analysis and *Other Works*, trans. J. Strachey. London: Hoghart Press, 1959.

Freud, S., *The Standard Edition of the Complete Psychological Works of Sigmund Freud Volume XXI (1927–1931): The Future of an Illusion, Civilization and its Discontents* and *Other Works*, trans. J. Strachey. London: Hoghart Press, 1961.

Freud, S., *The Standard Edition of the Complete Psychological Works of Sigmund Freud Volume XXII (1932–1936): New Introductory Lectures on Psycho-Analysis* and *Other Works*, trans. J Strachey. London: Hoghart Press, 1964.

Freud, S., *The Standard Edition of the Complete Psychological Works of Sigmund Freud Volume XXIII (1937–1939): Moses and Monotheism, An Outline of Psycho-Analysis,* and *Other Works*, trans. James Strachey. London: Hoghart Press, 1964.

Freud, S. & Binswanger, L., *The Sigmund Freud-Binswanger Correspondence*, trans. A. J. Pomerans. New York: Open Press, 2003.

Gay, P., *Freud. A Life for Our Time*. London: Papermac, 1988.

Heidegger, M., *Basic Question of Philosophy. Selected "Problems" of "Logic"*, trans. R. Rojcewicz & A. Schuwer. Cambridge: Bloomington/Indianapolis: Indiana University Press, 1994.

Heidegger, M., *Contributions to Philosophy (of the Event)*, trans. R. Rojcewicz & D. Vallega-Neu. Bloomington: Indiana University Press, 2012.

Heidegger, M., *Pathmarks*, trans. D. F. Krell. Cambridge: Cambridge University Press, 2009.

Heidegger, M., *Poetry, Language, Thought*, trans. A. Hofstadter. New York: Harper, 2001.

Herder, J. G., "Essay on the Origin of Language", trans. A. Gode. In Rosseau, J.-J., & Herder, A. G., *On the Origin of Language*. Chicago/London: University of Chicago Press, 1986.

Jones, E., *Sigmund Freud. Life and Work. Volume Three. The Last Phase 1919–1939*. London: Hoghart Press, 1957.

Joyce, J., *Finnegan's Wake*. Ware: Wordsworth, 2012.

Joyce, J., *Ulysses*. Ware: Wordsworth, 2010.

Kant, I., *Critique of Judgement*, trans. J. C. Meredith. Oxford/New York: Oxford University Press, 2008.

Kirk, G. S., Raven, J. E., & Schofield, M., *The Presocratic Philosophers*. Cambridge: Cambridge University Press, 2013.

Kojève, A., *Introductory Lectures on Hegel*, trans. J. H. Nichols Jr. Ithaca/London: Cornell University Press, 1980.

Lacan. J., *Écrits*, trans. B. Fink. New York/London: W.W. Norton & Company, 2006.

Lacan, J., "L'insu qui sait... Seminar XXIV. Final Sessions 1–12. 1976–1977", trans. C. Gallagher. http://www.lacaninireland.com/web/translations/seminars/.

Lacan, J., "RSI", trans. C. Gallagher. http://www.lacaninireland.com/web/translations/seminars/.

Lacan, J., *The Seminar of Jacques Lacan. Book I. Freud's Papers on Technique*, trans. J. Forrester. New York/London: W. W. Norton & Company, 1991.

Lacan, J., *The Seminar of Jacques Lacan. Book II. The Ego in Freud's Theory and in the Technique of Psychoanalysis*, trans. S. Tomascelli. New York/London: W. W. Norton & Company, 1991.

Lacan, J., *The Seminar of Jacques Lacan. Book IV. The Object Relation*, trans. A. R. Price. Cambridge: Polity, 2020.

Lacan, J., *The Seminar of Jacques Lacan. Book VI. Desire and its Interpretation*, trans. B. Fink. Cambridge: Polity Press, 2019.

Lacan, J., *The Seminar of Jacques Lacan. Book VII. The Ethics of Psychoanalysis*, trans. D. Porter. New York/London: W. W. Norton & Company, 1997.
Lacan, J., *The Seminar of Jacques Lacan. Book X. Anxiety*, trans. A. R. Price. Cambridge: Polity Press, 2020.
Lacan, J., *The Seminar of Jacques Lacan. Book XI. The Four Fundamental Concepts of Psychoanalysis*, trans. A. Sheridan. New York/London: W. W. Norton & Company, 1998.
Lacan, J., *The Seminar of Jacques Lacan. Book XX. On Feminine Sexuality, the Limits of Love and Knowledge*, trans. B. Fink. New York/London: W. W. Norton & Company, 1999.
Lacan, J., *The Seminar of Jacques Lacan. Book XXIII. The Sinthome*, trans. A. R. Price. Cambridge: Polity Press, 2016.
Lerner, P., "Beyond Silence: On the Absence of God in the Films of Ingmar Bergman." In *Psychoanalytic Perspectives on the Work of Ingmar Bergman: From Freud to Lacan and Beyond*, edited by Sinclair, V. New York/London: Routledge, 2022.
Lerner, P. "Bortom konstansprincipen." In *Freud och dödsdriften*, edited by Lerner, P. & Wessely, T. Simrishamn: TankeKraft, 2021.
Lerner, P. "The Pleasure Principle: The Epistemological Symptom of Psychoanalysis", *European Journal of Psychoanalysis* vol 8 nr 2 (2021).
Lucretius, *On the Nature of Things*, trans. C. Bailey. Oxford: Clarendon Press, 1910.
Matt, D. C., ed. *Zohar. Pritzker Edition. Volume One*, trans. D. C. Matt. Stanford: Stanford University Press, 2004.
Pascal, B., *Pascal's Pensées*, trans. W. F. Trotter. New York: Dutton, 1958.
Pessoa, F., *Livro do Desassossego por Bernando Soares*, Vol. I. Lisbon: Ática, 1982.
Plotinus, *The Enneads*, trans. S. MacKenna. London/New York: Penguin, 1991.
Rimbaud, A., *Je ne suis pas venu ici pour être heureux*. Paris: Flammarion, 2015.
Rubenstein, M.-J., *Strange Wonder. The Closure of Metaphysics and the Opening of Awe*. New York: Columbia University Press, 2008.
Rumi, J., *Essential Rumi*, trans. C. Barks. New Jersey: Castle Books, 1997.
Scholem, G., *Major Trends in Jewish Mysticism*. New York: Schocken, 1941.
Scholem, G., ed., *Zohar*. New York: Schocken, 1977.
Schreber, D. P., *Memoirs of My Nervous Illness*, trans. I. Macalpine & R. A. Hunter. New York: New York Review of Books, 2020.
Spinoza, B., *Ethics*, trans. E. Curley. London: Penguin, 1996.
Vico, G., *La Scienza Nuova e Opere scelte*. Turin: UTET, 1966.
Vico, G., *On the Most Ancient Wisdom of the Italians: Unearthed from the Origins of the Latin Language*, trans. L. M. Palmer. Ithaca/London: Cornell University Press, 1988.
Vico, G., *The New Science of Giambattista Vico*, trans. T. G. Bergin & M. H. Fisch. Ithaca/New York: Cornell University Press, 1948.
Vico, G., *New Science: Principles of the New Science Concerning the Common Nature of Nations*, trans. D. Marsh. London: Penguin, 2013.
Weil, S., *Gravity and Grace*, trans. E. Crawford & M. von der Rhur. London/New York: Routledge, 2003.
Winnicott, D., *Playing and Reality*. New York/London: Routledge, 2005.
Winnicott, D., *The Maturational Process and the Facilitating Environment: Studies in the Theory of Emotional Development*. London: Hoghart Press, 1965.
Wittgenstein, L., *Tractatus Logico-Philosophicus*, trans. C. K. Ogden. London: Kegan Paul, 1922.

Index

Note: Page numbers followed by "n" denote endnotes

al-Hallaj, Mansur 9, 64
animism 31–3, 35; and mourning 33–4; and poetic metaphysics 77–9
Aquinas, Thomas 59n47
awe 18, 50–4, 56, 58n32, 84

beauty 27–8, 34–5
being 45–7; essential occurrence of 51–4; and language 45–7, 57n16; subject of 47, 54; *see also* truth
Bion, Wilfred Rupert 7–8

Campi, Antonio 51–2
castration 29–30, 43–5, 94
clinamen 97–103
clinical structures 94–6, 96n5; autism 94–5; borderline 95; neurosis 95; neurotic substructures 19; paranoia 78; perversion 95; psychosis 85, 88n54, 95; schizoid 12, 19–20
creation: and being 54, 59n47; cosmogony 3, 5–6, 7, 9; and solitude 8, 17–18

Dalí, Salvador 59n48
death 33–7; death drive 27–8, 36–7
defense mechanisms: disavowal 91; intellectualization 10; negation 91; projection 32–3, 78; repression 43, 87n24, 91; splitting 91

Einstein, Albert 68–9n16
Empedocles 8
epistemological symptom (or repression) 30–1, 55–6, 67–8n3

ex nihilo 3, 5, 8, 22, 45, 55, 70–1
exile 2–3, 7–8; external 3–5, 12n5; internal 5–6

Heidegger, Martin 13n25, 45–8, 52–4
Herder, Johann Gottfried 83
holy 34–7

Ibn Arabi, Muhyiddin 9, 12n19, 12n20, 68n9, 69n17
intuition 5–6, 7, 10–11, 54–6, 63–4; and revelation 64–5

jouissance 43, 81–2, 93–4
Joyce, James 4, 24, 54–5, 76, 87n22

Kabbalah 2–3, 5–6, 68n7, 69n19
Kant, Immanuel 59–60n52
Kojève, Alexandre 61

lalangue 81–5
Luria, Isaac 2–3, 5–6, 7, 40n57

Meister Eckhart 9, 49
melancholia 19; narcissistic and schizoid 19, 28; *see also* mourning
metaontics 100–1
metaphor 82–3, 96n3; and divination 85–6; and metonymy 73–4, 79–82, 88n42, 91
mirror 16–17, 20–1, 50, 78, 84–6, 93–4; mirror stage 15, 82, 93
monotheism 56, 66; *Deus absconditus* 2, 49, 56; and interpretation 66;

Name-of-the-Father 42–4, 49; silence of God 49–51, 65
mother 16, 43, 85
mourning 25–7, 28–30, 36–7, 38n31; and melancholia 24–5
mystery (and enigma) *see truth*

narcissism 15, 24–5; primary and secondary 19, 94
nature of the unconscious 1, 49, 85, 104
neoplatonism 12–13n24, 58n28, 67–8n3
no one 6, 16–18, 21–3, 54–5

oceanic feeling 34–7, 39n53
Other of the Other 41–5, 49, 58n26, 84; and unimaginable 50

pantheism (or panentheism) 64–7
Pascal, Blaise 22, 49
Pessoa, Fernando 22–3
phallus 29–30, 94
play 16–18; melancholic 18–20
poetry 20–3, 35–6, 53–7, 83–6; and intimation 84–6; and music 22, 82, 84–5; poetic art of interpretation 10–11, 12n29; poetic logic 73–4, 79–83; poetic metaphysics 71–3, 76–9, 82–3; and prose 8, 79, 82
polytheism 34–7, 56, 66

quantum field theory 100–1

Rilke, Rainer Maria 27
Rimbaud, Arthur 9, 10, 21
rings: algebraic 90–2; Borromean 89–90; and voids 1, 92, 96, 103–4
Rumi, Jalal al-Din 9–10

Scholem, Gershom 12n1
Schreber, Daniel Paul 36, 78
solitude 6–11, 16–18, 22–3
Spinoza, Baruch 61–5, 100

truth 41–2; and being 44–5, 47–8, 51–4, 56; as cause 66–7; and enigma 48–9; and error 42–5, 49; and mysterious 51–4; and mystery 48–9; and rebus 49, 65; and revelation 49, 65–6, 69n18; and theistic structures 66–7

unimaginable 7, 10, 18, 20–1, 84–6, 96; indifferent 33–7; mysterious 49–54; Other of the Other 50; and unnameable 20, 56, 85

Vico, Giambattista 71, 75–6

Weil, Simone 13n24
Winnicott, Donald 8, 16–17
Wittgenstein, Ludwig 8, 65, 100